Private Label B

Startup Mistakes Private Label Business Owner Make, How to Prevent them and Grow Business

By

Amir Lime

Table of Contents

Dropshipping Business Model on a Budget

Private Label Crash Course

The 9+1 Best Home-Based Business Model of 2021

Bookkeeping and QuickBooks Made Easy

Bubble or Revolution? The Basics of Bitcoin and Blockchain.

Dropshipping Business Model on a Budget

The Risk-Low E-Com Guide to Create Your Online Store and Generate Profits with less than 47$

By

Amir Lime

Table of Contents

Introduction

With very little startup expenses, dropshipping is an innovative business model.

A dropshipping business is where an owner finds a collection of distributors to deliver and offer goods for their website. However, as in an e-commerce business, instead of owning the merchandise, a third party does much of the distribution and logistics for them. That third party is usually a wholesaler, who on behalf of the business "dropships" the consumer's goods.

When you start a retail shop, there are several factors to consider, but among the most significant aspects, you have to decide whether you'd like to store inventory or have a wholesale distributor. You must purchase goods in bulk, stock, unpack and send them to customers of your products if you want to store inventory. You may, therefore, contract the phase of storing, packaging and exporting to a drop-ship supplier by picking a wholesale distributor. As direct fulfillment, a drop-ship supplier is often described, but both definitions may be used to define the same service.

The wholesaler, who usually manufactures the product, delivers the product at the most basic, any time anyone buys a product, and you get a part of the sale for the product marketing.

Unless the client puts an order for it, you don't pay for the thing.

Dropshipping is an internet-based business model that draws novices and experts alike to choose a niche, create a brand, market and earn money, with probably the minimum entry barriers.

Chapter 1. What is Dropshipping?

Dropshipping is a retail model of e-commerce that enables retailers to offer goods without maintaining any physical inventory. The company sells the product to the buyer through dropshipping and sends the purchase order to a third-party seller, who then delivers the order directly on behalf of the retailer to the customer. Dropshipping sellers may not need to spend in any commodity stock, inventory or storage room and do not manage the phase of fulfillment.

Dropshipping is a form of retail fulfillment, where the goods are ordered from a third-party retailer instead of a store stocks products. The goods are then delivered directly to the customer. This way, the vendor doesn't have to personally manage the product. A familiar sound? Maybe not, but dropshipping is a fulfillment model utilized by 35 percent of online stores.

This is mostly a hands-off process for the store. The retailer doesn't have to buy stock or, in any manner, meet the orders. The third-party retailer, instead, takes control of the product itself.

For startups, dropshipping is great since it does not take as much as the conventional sales model. You don't have to prepare, pay overhead, & stock merchandise in a brick-and-mortar store. Instead, you start an online shop to purchase bulk goods and warehouse space from vendors that already have products.

In dropshipping, the merchant is solely responsible for attracting clients and handling orders, ensuring you'll be a middleman effectively. Despite this, through pricing up the goods you offer, you can gain the lion's share of the profits. It's an easy model of business, so one that can be really successful.

Millions of entrepreneurs switch to dropshipping to get started because it takes less hassle and capital. That's why you're probably interested. And the best of all news? Through dropshipping, you can create a company right from your laptop that is profitable in the long term.

There are several pitfalls and benefits, of course, and it is essential that we check at them before you launch your own e-commerce dropshipping firm. However, once you realize the positives and negatives of dropshipping, it'll be a breeze to learn how to do so effectively.

1.1 Benefits of dropshipping

For aspiring entrepreneurs, dropshipping is a smart business move to start with, which is accessible. You can easily evaluate multiple business concepts with a small downside with dropshipping, which helps you to think a lot about how to pick and sell in-demand goods. Here are a couple more explanations why dropshipping is a popular business.

1. Little capital is required

Perhaps the greatest benefit to dropshipping is that an e-commerce website can be opened without needing to spend thousands of dollars in stock upfront. Typically, retailers have had to bundle up large quantities of inventory with capital investments.

For the dropshipping model, unless you have already made the transaction and have been charged by the consumer, you may not have to buy a product. It is possible to start sourcing goods without substantial up-front inventory investments and launch a profitable dropshipping company with very little capital. And since you are not committed to sales, as in a typical retail sector, there is less chance of launching a dropshipping shop through any inventory bought up front.

2. Easy to get started

It's also simpler to operate an e-commerce company because you don't have to interact with physical products. You don't have to take stress with dropshipping about:

- Paying for a warehouse or managing it
- Tracking inventory for any accounting reasons
- Packing & shipping your orders
- Continually ordering products & managing stock level
- Inbound shipments and handling returns

3. Low overhead

Your overhead expenses are very minimal, and you don't have to deal with buying inventory or maintaining a warehouse. In reality, several popular dropshipping stores are managed as home-based enterprises, needing nothing more to run than a laptop & a few operational expenses. These costs are likely to rise as you expand but are still low relative to standard brick-and-mortar stores.

4. Flexible location

From almost anywhere via an internet connection, a dropshipping company can be managed. You can operate and manage the business as long as you can effectively connect with vendors and consumers.

5. Wide selection of goods to sell

Because you don't really have to pre-purchase any items you market, you can offer your potential clients a variety of trending products. If an item is stored by vendors, you will mark it for sale at no added cost at your online store.

6. Easier for testing

Dropshipping is a valuable form of fulfillment for both the opening of a new store and also for company owners seeking to measure consumers' demand for additional types of items, such as shoes or whole new product ranges. Again, the primary advantage of dropshipping is the opportunity to list and likely sell goods before committing to purchasing a significant quantity of stock.

7. Easier to scale

For a traditional retail firm, you would typically need to perform three times as much work if you get three times the amount of orders. By using dropshipping vendors, suppliers would be liable for more of the work to handle extra orders, helping you to improve with fewer growth pains & little incremental work.

Sales growth can often bring extra work, especially customer service, however companies which use dropshipping scale especially well comparison to standard e-commerce businesses.

8. Dropshipping starts easily.

In order to get started, you need not be a business guru. You don't really require some past company knowledge, honestly. You will get started easily and learn the rest while you move along if you spend some time to learn its basics.

It is too easy to drop shipping, and it takes so little from you. To help you out, you don't need a warehouse to store goods or a staff. You don't need to think about packaging or storage either. You do not even have to devote a certain period of time in your shop every day. Surprisingly, it's hands-off, especially once you get underway.

All of this means that today you can begin your company. Within a matter of hours, you will begin getting it up and running.

You're going to need some practical skills and the right equipment and tools. You will be equipped with the skills you have to jumpstart your own dropshipping company by the time you've done it.

9. Dropshipping grow easily.

Your business model doesn't even have to alter that much at all when you scale up. As you expand, you'll have to bring more effort into sales and marketing, but your daily life will remain almost the same.

One of the advantages of dropshipping is that when you scale, the costs do not spike. It's convenient to keep rising at a fairly high pace because of this. If you choose to build a little team at any stage, you can manage about anything by yourself, too.

10. Dropshipping doesn't need a big capital.

Since you need very little to start a dropshipping business, you can get underway with minimal funds. Right from your desktop, you can create a whole corporation, and you do not need to make any heavy investment. Your costs would be reasonably low even as your company grows, particularly compared to normal business expenses.

11. Dropshipping is flexible.

This is one of the greatest advantages. You get to be a boss of your own and set your own regulations. It's one of the most versatile occupations anyone can try.

With just a laptop, you can operate from anywhere, and you can operate at the hours that are most comfortable for you. For founders that want a company that fits for them, this is perfect. To get stuff done, you won't have to lean over backward. You choose your own pace instead.

Dropshipping is indeed flexible in that it allows you plenty of space to create choices that fit for you. Whenever you choose, you can quickly list new items, and you can change your plans on the move. You should automate it to work when you're gone, whether you're going on holiday. You get the concept prospects are limitless.

12. Dropshipping manages easily.

Because it doesn't need you to make several commitments, with no hassle, you can manage everything. When you have found and set up suppliers, you are often exclusively liable for your e-commerce store.

Chapter 2. How Dropshipping Works

Dropshipping functions by third-party suppliers, which deliver goods for each order on a just-in-time basis. When a sales order is received by the retailer, they transfer the requirements to the supplier—who manufactures the product.

While dropshipping is used by many e-commerce retailers as the base of their business processes, dropshipping can be used successfully to complement traditional retail inventory-stocking models. Because dropshipping does not create any unused surplus inventory, it may be used for analysis purposes before committing to sale on a marketplace, such as testing the waters.

Dropshipping works because, with the aid of a third party such as a wholesaler or an e-commerce shop, a dropshipper fulfills orders to deliver the goods for an even cheaper price. The majority of dropshippers offer goods directly from Chinese suppliers because the prices of most products in China are very poor. If the wholesaler's price is 5 dollars for a product. A dropshipper sells it for $8 and retains $3 for himself. The bulk of dropshippers target nations with higher purchasing power.

2.1 Awareness about the Supply Chain

You'll see the word "supply chain" a lot in here. It seems like a fancy lingo for the business, but it actually applies to how a product transfers from seller to consumer. We'll use this to explain the method of dropshipping.

2.2 The Supply Chain Process

You, the merchant, are only one puzzle piece. An effective dropshipping mechanism depends on several parties all acting in sync together. The supply chain is just that: producer, supplier, and retailer coordination.

You should split down the supply chain into three simple steps:

- The producer manufactures the goods and supplies them to wholesalers & retailers.

Let's say maker A is manufacturing bottles of water. They are marketed in bulk to manufacturers and wholesalers after the bottles come off the assembly line, who switch around & resell the bottles to dealers.

- Suppliers and wholesalers market the products to dealers.

For a particular type of product, a retailer like yourself is searching for a supplier. An arrangement to operate together is then reached between the retailer and the supplier.

A little point here: Although you may order directly from product producers, purchasing from retailers is always much cheaper instead. There are minimum purchasing criteria for most suppliers that can be very high, and you will still have to purchase stock & ship the goods.

So, purchasing directly from the producer might seem quicker, but you would profit more from buying from distributors (dealing with the little profit).

Suppliers are often convenient since all of them are skilled in a specific niche, so the type of items you need can be quickly identified. This also implies that you'll get started to sell super quick.

- Retailers sell goods to buyers.

Suppliers & wholesalers should not market to the public directly; that's the task of the retailer. The last move between the product & the consumer is the supplier.

Online stores from which customers buy goods are provided by retailers. The merchant marks it up again to reach at the final price after the wholesaler rates up the items. By "markup," we apply to fixing a premium that covers the product's cost price and gives you a benefit.

It's that! From start to end, it is the whole supply chain. In business, it's a simple but crucial concept.

You may have noted that no other group has been alluded to as a dropshipper. That is because there is no particular function for "dropshipper." Dropshipping is actually the activity of somebody else delivering goods. Technically, producers, retailers, and merchants will all be dropshippers.

Later on, we'll discuss how to start a retail dropshipping company in this guide. In other terms, you can learn how to become a trader who buys commodities from wholesalers to market to the public. This may indicate that through an online storefront, you sell through eBay or even your own website.

Remember what it's like for the consumer now that you realize what the supply chain is like.

2.3 What is Fulfillment?

Order fulfillment that's all the steps a corporation requires in having a fresh order and bringing the order into the hands of the customer. The procedure includes storing, picking & packaging the products, distributing them and sending the consumer an automatic email to let them know that the product is in transit.

2.4 The Steps to make Order Fulfillment

There are some steps involved in order fulfillment, which are as under:-

1. Receiving inventory.

Essentially, there are two approaches for an eCommerce company to manage inventory. It can decide to receive & stock the in-house inventory, or it can employ an outsourcer for eCommerce order fulfillment to take control of the inventory and other associated activities. The organization would be liable for taking stock, inspecting the product, marking, and maintaining the inventory method if it opts for the first alternative. If the business wishes to outsource or dropships, the order fulfillment agent or supplier can perform certain duties.

2. Storing inventory.

If you plan to stock the inventory yourself, after the receiving portion is finished, there'll be another list of assignments waiting for you. Shelving the inventory and holding a careful watch on what goods come in and what goods are going out would be the key activities on the list so that you can deliver the orders without any complications.

3. Processing the order.

Businesses who outsource order fulfillment do not have to get through the nitty-gritty of order delivery since they actually move on to their partner's order request and let them manage the rest. This is the phase where the order is taken off the shelves, shipped to a packaging station, examined for any damage, packed and transferred to the shipping station for businesses who handle their own product.

4. Shipping the order.

The best delivery strategy is calculated based on the scale, weight and precise specifications of the order. A third-party contractor is typically contracted to complete this phase.

Returns Handling. For online shoppers, the opportunity to refund unwanted goods quickly is a big factor in the purchase phase. You ought to design a crystal straightforward return policy that is readily available to all the customers and workers to ensure the receipt, repair and redemption of the returned goods are as successful as practicable. It will help you prevent needless confusion and errors by making this step automated.

Chapter 3. Why dropshipping is one of the best way to make money in 2021.

According to Forrester (analyst) Reports, the magnitude of online retail revenues would be $370 billion by the end of 2017. In comparison, 23 percent, which amounts to $85.1 billion, would come from dropshipping firms. To many businesses, like startups, this sheer scale alone is attractive.

An online retailer following this concept appears similar to its traditional e-commerce competitors by appearance. Dropshipping may be a well-kept mystery in the e-commerce world as consumers just think about the goods, price and credibility of the shop rather than how the goods are sourced and who delivers the shipments.

In summary,' dropshipping' is a business strategy in which the supplier does not directly hold the inventory or process the orders in his or her control. Both orders are delivered directly from a wholesaler and delivered. This encourages the supplier to concentrate on the business's selling aspect.

Many major e-commerce names, such as Zappos, began with dropshipping. For those that seek motivation, billion-dollar dropshipping internet store Wayfair or the milliondollarBlinds.com are top examples today.

Five explanations of how the dropshipping business strategy appeals to both startups and experienced entrepreneurs are offered below. These issues in traditional e-commerce have been nagging challenges, which can be addressed with the dropshipping model immediately.

3.1 Dropshipping Is The E-Commerce Future

It seem that dropshipping will be the future of e-commerce. Here are some main reasons which explain this concept.

Sourcing of Product:

Conventional e-commerce stores must directly import supplies from wholesalers, frequently based in various countries. They often need goods to be bought in bulk and are then shipped prior to being promoted and distributed to the local warehouse. A lot of time, money & resources are required for the whole phase. The presence of expensive intermediaries, such as banks, freight shipments and export-import brokers, also involves it.

The dropshipping model, however, enables manufacturers to market goods for large quantities of each product without needing to think about sourcing. The entire method is substantially simplified with just a turn-key e-commerce storefront such as Shopify and a dropshipping software like Oberlo. The retailer may choose to notify the distributors via e-mail to tell them that their supplies are now being shipped to the store. The most of the procedure can be quickly handled from the dashboard, such as uploading product images, updating pricing and order monitoring.

Storage

A traditional e-commerce store, particularly as it carries multiple or large products, requires large storage spaces. It might be imaginable to store ten to 100 items, but storing 1,000 or 1,000,000 items will cost a real fortune that is not within the reach of a start-up. This high warehouse rent issue is addressed by the dropshipping model since the goods remain with the distributor or wholesale retailer until they are bought.

Order fulfillment

Many pioneers of e-commerce do not foresee investing most of their time picking, packaging and delivering orders. They should, of course, outsource the order fulfillment for ease to a boutique e-commerce fulfillment, such as ShipMonk. The dropshipping model, however, facilitates hands-free shipment, since the whole packaging and shipping process is in the possession of the wholesaler or distributor.

Cataloging & photography

A conventional e-commerce shop owner has to take professional-quality images of items that may be very pricey, like a decent digital camera, a light panel, lighting and some more. For a dropshipping control software, this issue is fixed, as the "product importing" function allows for instant picture import.

Scalability

Wayfair.com is a major online dropshipping store that holds 10,000 vendors of more than eight million items. Yes, $8 million. By this business model, such huge scalability is made possible.

Because the retailer just has to work on the publicity and customer care aspect, they don't have to think about the warehouse's rent and other operating expenses skyrocketing.

In conclusion, the dropshipping paradigm offers the ability for tiny startups with minimal capital to contend with large and medium online stores comfortably, rendering the field of e-commerce an equal environment for everyone. That being said, plan in the future to see more e-commerce shops adopting this model.

Chapter 4. Niche And Product Selection

You want a business to start, but the thing that holds you down is the market niche that you feel you need to pick. And, honestly, it can be tricky: you might mention all your interests & passions and yet feel like you haven't hit the singular thing that you were expected to do.

Yet, it can trigger paralysis to place some sort of burden on yourself to choose the very right niche.

Certainly, in choosing a suitable niche business, you like to do your careful research, but it's easier to get up and run than to wait around. You will try ideas that way, enter the market earlier, and benefit from the victories and losses. That way, too, you can still take what you have gained from previous attempts, so step on with fresh concepts if the first company does not take off.

4.1 Steps how to search your right niche

Using the following five methods to find your niche, whether you're unable to determine or you need more information to work with.

1. Identify your interests & passions.

This could be something that you have achieved before. But, if you haven't, quickly make a compilation of 10 topical passions and areas of passion.

Business isn't easy, and it can challenge you at any stage. If you work in an area you don't care for, the likelihood of leaving will increase significantly—especially like a first sole proprietor.

This doesn't mean that a better match has to be found. You can stay with it if you are excited about any part of running the business. If you don't care about the issue, you might not be able to easily find the drive to persevere within.

2. Identify problems that you can solve.

You're able to get to narrow down your choices with your list of ten topics in hand. You first need to identify challenges that your target clients are facing to build a viable enterprise, then decide if you can potentially fix them. Here are a few items you should do to find issues in different niches.

3. Research your competition.

There is not always a bad thing in the presence of competition. It can actually show you that you've discovered a market that's lucrative. Although you do have to do an in-depth analysis of competing pages. Build a fresh spreadsheet and start tracking all the competing websites that you can find.

And find out whether there's already an opening in the crowd to stick out. Are you still willing to rate the keywords? Is there really a way to distinguish and build a unique offer for yourself? Here are some indications that you will enter a niche and flourish, even though it is already covered by other sites:

- Content of poor quality. In a niche where several company owners are not delivering high-quality, informative content that suits the viewer, it's easy to outrank the competitors.
- Lack of transparency. By establishing an authentic and accessible identity in a niche where most platforms are faceless and unnecessarily corporate, many internet marketers have disrupted whole industries.
- The lack of paid competitiveness. If you have noticed a keyword with a relatively high search rate but little competition with paying ads, there is undoubtedly a potential for you to upset the business.

4. Determine the profitability of the niche.

You need to have a fairly decent understanding now about what niche you're about to get into. You might not have limited your selection down to a particular region of the topic, but you've certainly noticed a few suggestions that you feel pretty good about. It's important to have an idea at this stage about how much money you have the opportunity to make in your niche. A fine way to go to continue your search is ClickBank.

So, browse the category's best brands. That is not a positive indication if you can't locate any offers. It could mean that the niche could not be monetized by someone.

You're in luck if the quest throws up a good amount of products – just not an excessive amount of products. Take notice of pricing points such that your own goods can be marketed in a fair way.

Bear in mind, though, that you may not have to launch your organization with your own product offering. You should collaborate in your niche with product makers, marketers and site owners to start earning commissions when working on your innovative solution.

5. Test your idea.

You are now prepared with all the knowledge you need to pick a niche, and checking your proposal is the only thing needed to do. Setting up a landing page for pre-sales of a product you're producing is one easy way to do this. Through paying ads, you will then push traffic to this page.

That doesn't actually mean that you are not in a viable niche, even though you don't get pre-sales. Your message may not be quite correct, or you haven't found the right deal yet. You will maximize conversions by using A/B split testing to figure out whether there is something preventing the target group from taking action or not.

You will sell to two fundamental markets: customer and corporation. Such divisions are reasonably clear. "For example, if you sell women's clothes from a department shop, shoppers are your target market; if you sell office supplies, companies are your target market (this is referred to as "B2B" sales). In certain instances, for example, you could be selling to both corporations and people if you operate a printing company.

No company, especially a small one, can be everything to all individuals. The more you can describe your target group broadly, the stronger. For even the larger corporations, this method is recognized as building a market and is crucial to growth. Walmart and Tiffany are also stores, but they have somewhat different niches: Walmart caters to bargain-minded customers, while Tiffany tends to luxury jewelry buyers.

"Some entrepreneurs make the error of slipping into the "all over the map" pit instead of building a niche, believing they can do many things and be successful at all of them. Falkenstein warns that these individuals soon learn a difficult lesson: "Smaller is larger in market, and smaller is not across the map; it is extremely focused."

4.2 Creating a good niche

Keep in mind these important to create a good niche:

1. Make a wish list.

Who do you like to do business with? Be as descriptive as you are capable of. Identify the regional spectrum and the kinds of firms or clients that you want your organization to target. You can't make contact if you do not really know whom you are going to do business with. Falkenstein cautions, "You must recognize that you can't do business with everyone." Otherwise, you risk leaving yourself exhausted and confusing your buyers.

The trend is toward small niches these days. It's not precise enough to target teens; targeting adult, African American teenagers with the family incomes of $40,000 or more is. It is too large to target corporations that market apps; it is a better aim to target Northern California-based firms that offer internet software distribution and training that have sales of $15 million or more.

2. Focus.

Clarify what you intend to sell, knowing that a) to all customers, you can't be all items and b) smaller is better. Your specialty isn't the same as that of sector you are employed in. A retail apparel corporation, for example, is not a niche but a sector. Maternity clothes for corporate mothers" may be a more specific niche."

Using these strategies to assist you in starting this focus process:

- Create a compilation of the greatest activities you do and the talents that are inherent in many of them.
- List your accomplishments.
- Identify the important things of life that you've experienced.
- Look for trends that reflect your personality or approach to addressing issues.

Your niche should emerge from your desires and expertise in a normal way. For instance, if you spent 10 years of working in such a consulting firm and also ten years working for such a small, family-owned company, you may actually have to start a consulting company that specializes in limited, family-owned businesses.

3. Describe the customer's worldview.

A good corporation utilizes what Falkenstein called the Platinum Rule: "Do to the others as they're doing to themselves." You will define their desires or desires as you look at the situation from the viewpoint of your prospective clients. Talking to new clients and recognizing their biggest issues is the perfect approach to achieve this.

4. Synthesize.

Your niche can begin to take shape at this point when the opinions and the desires of the consumer and desire to coalesce to create something different. There are five attributes of a Strong Niche:

- In other terms, it relates to your long-term view and carries you where you like to go.
- Somebody else needs it, consumers in particular.
- It is closely arranged.
- It's one-of-a-kind, "the only city game."
- It evolves, enabling you to build multiple profit centers and yet maintain the core market, thus guaranteeing long-term success.

5. Evaluate.

It is now time to test the product or service proposed against the five requirements in Phase 4. Perhaps you'll notice that more business travel than that you're ready for is needed for niche you had in mind. That indicates that one of the above conditions is not met-it will not carry you where you like to go. Scrap it, and pass on to the next proposal.

6. Test.

Test-market it until you have a balance between the niche and the product. "Give individuals an opportunity to purchase your product or service, not just theoretically, but actually put it out there." By giving samples, such as a complimentary mini-seminar or a preview copy of the newsletter, this can be accomplished. "If you spend enormous sums of cash on the initial trial run, you're possibly doing it wrong," she says. The research shouldn't cost you a bunch of money:

7. Go for it!

It is time for your idea to be implemented. This is the most challenging step for many entrepreneurs. But worry not: if you have done your research, it would be a measured risk to reach the business, not simply a chance.

Chapter 5. How to start dropshipping business in 2021

It's not easy to learn the way to start a dropshipping company, as with any type of business. Nevertheless, it's a perfect first move in the world of business. Without keeping any inventory, you may sell to customers. You do not have to pay upfront for goods. And if you are passionate about your new venture, in the long term, you will create a sustainable source of revenue.

In this complete dropshipping guide, suggest taking the following market and financial moves if you are considering dropshipping.

Others are mandatory from the start, and others are only a smart idea, so it will save you time and stress down the line by coping with them up front.

Dropshipping is a method of order fulfillment that helps shop owners to deliver without stocking any stock directly to buyers. If a consumer orders a commodity from a dropshipping shop, it is delivered directly to them by a third-party retailer. The client pays the selling price that you set, you pay the market price of the vendors, and the rest is benefit. You never need to maintain goods or spend in inventory.

You are responsible for designing a website and your own label, as well as selecting and promoting the items you choose to offer in the dropshipping business strategy. Your corporation is therefore liable for the expense of shipping and for setting rates that result in a reasonable profit margin.

Steps For Starting A Dropshipping Profitable Business

Learn to find high-margin products, introduce them to your business, and easily begin selling them.

1. Commit yourself for starting a dropshipping business

Dropshipping, as in any other business, needs considerable effort and a long-term focus. You're going to be deeply surprised if you're looking for a six-figure benefit from 6 weeks of part-time employment. You would be far less likely to get frustrated and leave by entering the organization with reasonable assumptions regarding the commitment needed and the prospects for benefit.

You'll need to spend heavily when beginning a dropshipping venture, utilizing one of the two following currencies: time or funds.

Investing time in dropshipping business

Our recommended strategy, particularly for the first dropshipping developers, is bootstrapping & investing sweat equity to develop your company. For various factors, we prefer this method over spending a huge amount of money:

- You will understand how the organization works inside out, which, as the enterprise expands and scales, will be crucial for handling others.

- You would know your clients and business personally, helping you to make smarter choices.
- You would be less inclined to waste huge amounts on vanity ventures that are not vital to success.
- You will build some new talents that will enable you a stronger entrepreneur.

Realistically, most persons are not ready to leave their work in order to ramp up their own online shop for six months. It might be a little more complicated, but even though you're already doing a 9-to-5 job, it's surely feasible to get underway with dropshipping, assuming you set reasonable standards for your customers about customer support and delivery times. When you continue to expand, as much as working capital and profitability allow, you will move into working long hours on your company.

Both companies and entrepreneurs are specific, but it is feasible to produce a monthly income stream of $1,000-$2,000 within 12 months of working around 10 to 15 hours per week to develop the firm.

Excited regarding starting a new business but not knowing where to begin? This informative guide will show you how to identify great products with strong sales potential that are newly trendy.

If you have the choice of working long hours on your company, that's the best option to increase your profit prospects and the possibility of good dropshipping. It is particularly beneficial in the early days to concentrate all the energies on publicity when creating traction is essential. It would normally take approximately 12 months of full-time jobs based on our knowledge, with a heavy focus on publicity for a dropshipping firm to replace an annual full-time salary of $50,000.

For a very small payout, it might sound like a lot of work, but bear these two points in mind:

When the dropshipping company is up and going, it would actually require considerably less time than from a 40-hour-per-week work to maintain it. In terms of the reliability and scalability that the dropshipping paradigm offers, much of your expenditure pays off.

You establish more than just a revenue stream when you develop a company. You also build an asset that you will market in the future. Be sure that when looking at the true return, you remember the equity valuation you are accruing, and also the cash flow produced.

Investing money in dropshipping business

By spending a lot of capital, it is feasible to develop and grow a dropshipping company, but we suggest against it. We attempted all methods to growing an enterprise (bootstrapping it ourselves vs. outsourcing the procedure), and while we were in the trenches doing much of the work, we had the most progress.

In the early stages, it is vital to have someone who is profoundly involved in the company's future to construct it from the ground up. You would be at the hands of pricey engineers, developers, and advertisers who will easily eat away whatever money you produce without knowing how your organization operates at any stage. You don't have to do everything it yourself, but at the start of your company, we highly advocate becoming the primary motivating power.

To have your company started and operating, you would, though, require a modest cash reserve in the $1,000 range. For limited administrative costs (like web hosting and dropshipping providers), you may need this and to pay some incorporation fees, which we will cover below.

2. Dropshipping business idea to chose

The second phase in studying how to launch a dropshipping company is to do the market research required. You want to find a niche you are interested in and make choices based on how effective it can be, almost like though you were starting a grocery shop and checking at the numerous sites, rivals, and developments. But the fact is, it's tricky to come up with product concepts to offer.

Niche goods also have a more passionate client base, which, through increasing awareness about the items, will make marketing to unique audiences simpler. A good entry point to begin dropshipping without cash could be health, clothes, makeup goods, appliances, phone accessories, or yoga-related pieces.

Any instances of dropshipping stores in a niche may be:

- Dog bow and ties for dog lovers
- Exercise equipment for fitness
- iPhone cases and cables for iPhone owners
- Camping gear for campers

To try the dropshipping business ideas, you may also use the appropriate techniques:

Google Trends could really help you identify whether, as well as the seasons in which they tend to trend, a product is trending up or down. Notice the search volume is not indicated by Google Patterns. But if you're using it, be sure to use a keyword tool such as Keywords Everywhere to cross-check your data to determine the popularity of the product in search.

3. Do competitor research

You want to check about your competitors so that you know what you're trying to sell in your shop and appreciate the way they operate. Your competitors may have great success hints which can help you develop a better marketing strategy for your dropshipping firm.

Limit your study to only five other dropshipping firms, like one or two major players such as Walmart or Ebay, if your business has a number of competitors (that is a positive thing in dropshipping). It will help you remain centered and prepare your next phase.

4. Choose a dropshipping supplier

Choosing a supplier for dropshipping is a crucial move towards creating a profitable dropshipping business. A dropshipping company does not have any goods to ship to consumers without vendors and would thus cease to operate.

At this stage, you analyzed what goods you want to offer and realize that they can be profitable, and you want to know where to find a provider of dropshipping that provides you with the high-quality service that you need to grow. By linking Oberlo to the online store, eCommerce platforms such as Shopify provide a plug-and-play style alternative to find possible suppliers.

5. Build your ecommerce store

An eCommerce platform such as Shopify is the next what you need to launch a dropshipping business. This is the home where you deliver traffic, offer goods, and payments are processed.

These type of platforms makes the e-commerce website simple to create and launch. It is a complete commerce service that connects you to sell and receive payments in several ways, like online, sell in different currencies, and conveniently manage products.

To use e-commerce websites, you don't need to become a programmer or developer either. They have resources to assist with anything from domain name ideas to logo design, and with the store creator and Payment processing themes, you are quickly able to modify the feel and look of your store.

6. Market your dropshipping store

It's time to talk about promoting your new shop, now that you know to start a dropshipping firm. You may want to bring more work into your marketing and promotional activities while developing the dropshipping business strategy to stick out in your market.

You will invest time working on selling and supporting the company in the following ways, with too many stuff about dropshipping being processed:

- Paid ads (Facebook & Google).

For a Facebook ad, the average cost is about 0.97 cents per click, that's not too bad if you're new to social media advertising. Facebook ads are extensible, goods can perform ok on them, and they click into the desire of people to purchase momentum. You can run Google Shopping Ads and target lengthy keywords that are more likely to be purchased by shoppers. Typically, with Google ads, there is more price competition, but it might be worthy of your time to check it out.

- Influencer marketing.

You may have a low funds for marketing your business as a new dropshipper. Influencer marketing is also an affordable way to target audience because individuals are more likely than traditional advertising to trust influencers. When you go this route, start negotiating an affiliate fee versus a flat rate with the influencer. It's a win-win situation, as every sale they're going to make money off, and the cost is going to be less for you.

- Mobile marketing.

Smartphone marketing is a broad term referring to a company that connects with clients on their mobile phones. You can start with a VIP text club, for example, and encourage website users to sign up for the exclusive promotions & deals. Or provide client support through Messenger in a live chat session with shoppers. You can create automated qualified leads, customer loyalty, and cart abandonment campaigns with a mobile marketing tool such as ManyChat to drive sales and profits for your dropshipping business.

Stay updated on what channels are operating and which are not, as with any profitable online business, especially if you invest money in them like paid ads. You can always adjust your marketing plan to lower costs as well as maximize revenue as you keep growing and improve your business.

7. Analyze your offering

You should start looking at the consequences of your diligent work after you've been promoting and operating your dropshipping company for some time. Any analytics will help you address some critical online shop queries, like:

- Sales

What are my channels with the highest performance? Where am I expected to put more ad dollars? What else are my favorite items for sale? What are my greatest clients?

- Behavior of shoppers

Do citizens buy more on their laptops or cell phones? For each unit, what's the conversion rate?

- Margins of profit

Why are the most profitable pieces and variant SKUs? What do my month-over-month revenue and gross income look like?

To track web traffic over time and optimize your search engine optimization activities, you can even use resources like Google

Analytics & Search Console. Plus, you review the results monthly to guarantee that your overall plan succeeds with your business, whether you are utilizing third-party software for your social network or messenger marketing.

You want to build a data-informed analytics framework while building a dropshipping e-commerce store. Remain compatible with what you evaluate over time and calculate the consistency of your store against simple KPIs. This will encourage you to make better choices for your store, so move your small business over time to the next level.

Chapter 6. How To identify Best Suppliers For Your New Dropshipping Business

Dropshipping is a model for eCommerce that is increasingly attractive. That is because launching a dropshipping company is simpler (not to say less expensive) than managing inventory for a traditional digital storefront.

The whole model of drop shipment is focused on the retailer doing its job well and delivering orders timely and effectively. It goes without saying, therefore, that identifying the appropriate supplier is one, if not the most important, and a step towards creating a successful brand. If an order is messed up by your supplier/seller, you and your organization are liable, so the trick is to find someone who adheres to the schedule and is open to discuss any problems

The advantages and disadvantages of dropshipping are well known, but it has become far less obvious that the most significant part of beginning a dropshipping business is choosing the right vendors for your WooCommerce shop. Until now.

6.1 The Importance of Selecting The Right Suppliers

A special model for eCommerce is Dropshipping. To retain their own inventories, conventional online retailers compensate. Those expenses are all but offset by dropshipping, so dropshipping would not need substantial start-up investment.

In the other side, dropshipping suggests that you place the destiny of your eCommerce store in the possession of others.

With the dropshipping system, retailers focus on wholesalers, manufacturers, and dealers who meet the orders of the retailers.

The dropshipping puzzle has several parts, and for the greater image, each component is critical. Among those pieces, one of the most significant is dropshipping suppliers. In reality, the finest dropshippers know that a dropshipping eCommerce store can make or break the efficiency and overall reliability of dropshipping suppliers.

6.2 Finding Your Dropshipping Suppliers

It needs you to partner with manufacturers, wholesalers, & distributors to start a dropshipping business. You want to identify vendors who improve the dropshipping business rather than compromise it.

Research Your Products

You have to figure out what types of things you can sell before you can start finding and working with vendors.

You want to address queries in specific, such as:

- Where does the item come from?
- How long would manufacturing take?
- How is it done?

Are there factors of height or weight which might make fulfillment more complicated or more costly?

The purpose is not expertise; however, you want to get to know the goods so that you can help determine which ones are suitable for dropshipping.

Understand the supply chain and recognize the considerations

You need to get familiar with dropship supply chain after nailing down your goods. In other terms, you should to know how it works for dropshipping.

For dropshipping, the items never really go into the hands of the dealer. Instead, an order is issued by the retailer, and a supplier who manages packing and delivery initiates fulfillment. In this way, the dealer is like the director of a dropshipping company.

You can't sell goods if you don't have reputable vendors, which suggests that you don't have a dropshipping business.

You need to get familiar with dropship supply chain since nailing down your products. In other terms, you need to understand how it functions for dropshipping.

For dropshipping, the items never really go into the hands of the dealer. Instead, an order is issued by the retailer and a supplier who manages packing and delivery initiates fulfilment. In this manner, the retailer is just like the director of a dropshipping company.

You can't sell goods if you don't have reputable suppliers, which suggests that you don't have a dropshipping business.

Search for Dropshipping Wholesalers on Google

You will identify the major vendors for your preferred commodities or product types with a Google search.

When you build a preliminary list, by studying the next few queries, take notice of the various characteristics of dropshipping suppliers.

- What is supplier location?
- Will the retailer link with your WooCommerce shop so that fresh orders are immediately submitted for fulfillment?
- What (if any) is the sum of minimum order (MOQ)?
- What support (e.g., mobile, email, chat, etc.) does the provider offer?
- What kind of range of items does the retailer offer?

Subscribe to Dropshipping Suppliers Directories

And if lots of choices pop up in the Google searches, directories will bring even more options. For a broad selection of items, these repositories comprise of web lists of dropshipping vendors and wholesalers.

You should recognize that some of the finest are premium directories, such as Salehoo and Worldwide Labels, implying they need paying subscriptions. There are a lot of free directories accessible that you can access at no fee, like Wholesale Central. Free directories, though, are occasionally obsolete. Newer vendors do not exist, and suppliers are also listed who are no longer in operation.

Usually, premium directories vary in cost from $20 a month for lifetime access to a few hundred bucks. You can find the expense of a premium directory to be beneficial, with free directories often hit-or-miss. There are also premium directories, like Doba, explicitly customized for dropshipping.

Figure Out Your Competitor's Suppliers

It follows that you must see what your competitors do if you want to be successful in the dropshipping field. Do any acknowledgment, in fact, to see which manufacturers are meeting their requirements.

There are a lot of methods to do this, but testing the markets that the competitors sell is the best.

If the supplier is not listed on the page, by making your own order, you will always show the supplier. Since the retailer is pleased, an invoice or packaging slip from them would possibly be included with the shipment. To ask about a partnership with your own dropshipping company, you can then contact the supplier directly.

Attend Trade Seminars

Trade shows have been considered to be an efficient place for manufacturers to set up and grow their companies. So, if you haven't been to a trade seminar yet, add it to the end of the list of to-do events.

You network with other participants within dropship supply chain, like distributors and dropshipping wholesalers, at trade shows. You get an insider's view on current and future products that you should introduce to your online store. For dropshipping businesses, you even get to "talk shop" face-to-face, which is also the most successful way to do business.

Join Industry Groups and Networks

Trade shows facilitate with locating vendors for dropshipping firms, yet another effective resource is business networks and groups.

The majority of retailers, like the identities of their dropshipping vendors, are not willing to share the secrets of their performance. The individuals who enter business groups, however, want to share, learn, & develop. Through being part of the dropshipping network, you will get valuable insight from industry professionals. Your colleagues, for instance, might recommend better suppliers or alert you about suppliers in order to avoid.

Connect with the Manufacturers

Not all manufacturers supply to consumers directly, although there are those who do. Until picking vendors for your eCommerce dropshipping shop, suggest reaching out to the producers of the goods that you will market.

You have far higher margins when a producer chooses to be the distributor than with a traditional retailer or wholesaler. Manufacturers, on the other hand, frequently impose minimum order amounts that could need bigger orders. You might find yourself with considerable inventory to deal in this situation, which is intended to circumvent dropshipping.

Ask the vendor to recommend vendors for you if a manufacturer won't work with you. A recommendation, after all, indicates that the agreements and commitments between a manufacturer and a supplier is successful. For that cause, it is definitely worth putting suggested vendors on your list of possibilities.

Order Samples

There's no substitution for firsthand knowledge, no matter how many feedback or testimonials you find. This is why ordering samples is the next phase in finding the correct dropshipping suppliers for the business.

Ordering samples teaches you a few key things about a supplier. First one is that you get to know the product's consistency yourself.

The second is that you will see how delivery is done by the retailer, and what shipment packaging seems to if a different vendor is involved, and how long it takes to ship and distribute. Suppliers will execute the requests, so buying samples provides you with an idea of what your clients will feel.

Confirm Contract Terms & Fees

You compiled several options, removed any but the most suitable possibilities, ordered tests to assess certain vendors, and decided on your dropshipping company with the right supplier (or suppliers). Negotiating deal conditions and payments is the last option left to do.

New businesses with unproven consumer bases have fewer bargaining leverage relative to mature companies with established customer bases. When it comes to communicating the margins, this is especially true.

Since dropshipping means that you don't have to hold your inventory, there would be low margins. The bulk of inventory costs and expenditures involved with meeting your orders is borne by your supplier(s). With dropshipping, because prices are smaller, gross margins are often lower than if you stored and delivered orders personally.

With margins generally poor, the fees concerned may be the biggest distinction between vendors. Such suppliers, for instance, charge flat per-order rates that are applied to the overall cost of the goods. Per-order payments typically vary from $2 and $5 to cover delivery and shipping costs (although big or unwieldy goods can require higher fees).

In the end, you want to select the supplier(s) that satisfies your specifications and give contracts of appropriate terms.

Chapter 7. Setting Up Your Dropshipping business On A Budget

The establishment of a dropshipping company as an eCommerce business is a perfect way to earn money. Managing a business without the hassle of product and shipping logistics is the most convincing aspect of a dropshipping store

You have already heard stories from businessmen about how costly it is to start a business. This involve accounts of hopelessly pursuing buyers or firms failing because of bleak financials to remain afloat. Do not let this scare you from launching a dropshipping store, as this model enables you to offer low-risk products.

What you need to do is get the orders and call the supplier-the rest is up to them.

There are very few financial barriers associated with the establishment of a dropshipping store when it comes to financing the company. In fact, with around zero initial investment, you can get underway with an online store.

Here's a 7-step feasible plan for launching a dropshipping shop on a budget shoestring.

1. Research Your Options

You'll need to do some research before beginning some form of business.

It requires getting online and finding out the competitors that offer related goods. To see just what each has to suggest, you'll also want to spend a little time investigating the future vendors and distributors.

Each shipping group will have a specific way of doing stuff and pricing models, therefore pay careful attention to those specifics so that you can ensure that you team up with your dropshipping store with the right party.

2. Create a Plan to Stick

You'll need to get a solid plan in progress before you can launch your business activities. A budget is used with this. It's important to decide what your budget is, whether you have $100 or $500 to get underway and ensure that you adhere to it. The easiest way to achieve so is to maintain good track of all your spending to guarantee that as you start up your store, you do not go over the budget.

3. Find Your Niche

In reality, many believe that it is an impossible task. It may be really challenging to appeal to all. Instead, rather than attempting to market could product under the sun, choose the goods focused on a particular niche.

Select a particular area of the business, such as organic pet food or dog clothes, if you decide that you want to market animal-related items.

When you can refine your attention down, you can have a much higher sales rate, and you are more likely to be noticed when customers are looking for a particular form of a product. Your small shop can get lost in the noise of competitors if your focus is too big.

4. Set Up Your eCommerce website

This is the phase through which you finally launch and set up your site with a dropshipping store.

Three of the most successful eCommerce sites accessible to sellers today are Shopify and Wix. It's quick to get started, as well as its user-friendly interface, also for sellers who are not especially tech-savvy, makes configuration and maintenance easy.

With monthly prices of less than $40, Shopify and Wix are both inexpensive alternatives, making it a perfect way to get off on a budget in the digital marketplace. You may also open a Modalyst store to boost the delivery and streamline the distribution process.

You're able to move on to the next stage after you have set up a simple online storefront that has your products selected.

5. Make Meetings With Your Suppliers

When it comes to choosing which provider to use it for your dropshipping shop, there are lots of decisions out there. Because you've done your homework in phase one already, now is the moment where your decision is formalized. Through entering into a contract with the commodity distributor(s) of your choosing, you will do so. Any of the most successful shipping partners makes it simple to get started, and in no time, unlike having to pay such upfront costs, you will be on your way.

The most relevant issues you are asking your prospective suppliers are:

- Do you keep all products in stock?
- How do you care the returns?
- What is your normal or average processing time?
- In which areas do you ship to? Do international shipping available?
- What kind of support did you offer?
- Is there any limit for orders?

You would have a solid understanding about how your suppliers conduct their company until you meet a supplier who addresses certain questions to your satisfaction. In addition, as a seller dealing for them, you'll realize what you need to do. You're on the path to a successful working partnership at this point.

6. Start Selling

Oh, congratulations. In launching your online store, this is one of most exciting steps. It's time to add your product details to your website and start selling until you have all your arrangements and agreements in order.

If customers are not aware of the products, you will not have enough sales, to begin with. You'll want to waste more time and money on ads if this is the case. By beginning with low-cost advertisements on Instagram and Facebook, or advertising on blogs as well as other websites which have a common audience, you will keep advertising costs reasonably small.

7. Optimize Your Site

You should take some time to customize the website until you have some revenue and knowledge under your belt. You can do all this earlier in the process, but waiting to see what is really working before you start to make changes is often a good idea.

There are a broad variety of customization choices for sites such as Shopify and Modalyst, including templates that change the way your website looks and plugins to can customize how your website works. The primary aim here is to tweak the site in ways that make it smoother for your clients and more organized.

As you've seen, all it takes to set up an online store is a few steps, and most of them don't need any money. You're not lonely if you're excited about being an owner of an eCommerce company just don't have a ton of money to launch with. This is why so many platforms are accessible that make it easier to get started without investing a million in the process.

Making sure that it works and prepare a strategy that you will use to guide you when keeping under your budget by setting up your dropshipping business, no matter how small it might be.

Chapter 8. Mistakes To Avoid When Developing Your Dropshipping Business

In an environment that jumps at the chance to make a business deal quick and convenient, Dropshipping tends to have a no for retailers. It might seem like, now, acquiring the goods and marketing with a bit of savvy are your only worries. Yet, if you wish to hold the company afloat, you should not forget about the client's perspective. True, the boring duties of inventory, order filling, and then ensuring shipping can be passed on.

The dropshipping company, however, does not waste any time thinking about the feelings of your client. How do you assume if your client is going to be satisfied? The buyers are the ones who put the money back. Anything falls out the window if they're not satisfied. You would need to consider the duties and what failures typically trigger it all to backfire in order to completely enjoy the advantages of utilizing dropshipping.

Here are a common mistake that leads to the failure end of your dropshipping business, so you should hold these mistakes in mind all the time.

1. Worrying About Shipping Costs.

While shipping costs might be a doozy, it's never productive to stress. In this area, you will need to decide under which your priorities lie. Shipping prices can vary all over the board, depending on where orders come from. This stress can be relieved by setting a flat rate and generally evens out with time. Not only does this make things easier for you, but it's also simple and easy for customers.

2. Relying Much on Vendors.

By putting much trust in such a vendor, a good number of crises can arise. For example, they may go out of business or increase their rates on you if you only use one vendor. They might run out of the items that you expect them to supply. Where would you be then? This is why there should always be a backup for you. It is smart to write up the contract with your vendors for your own insurance to remain aware of your requirements. This will ensure that everyone involved has agreed to uphold what you demand.

3. Expecting Easy Money.

Dropshipping, as we've already established, offers a degree of ease that can seem to make your work easier. Yet, you can't ignore how critical your product is in marketing and all the competition you're going to face. This involves analysis and the creation of a unique approach that will allow the product more attractive than that of anyone else.

4. Making Order Difficult to Access.

When you assure your consumers a simple and quick procedure, they'll want to see the proofs. Set approximate location-based ship dates and require suppliers to keep you posted on the status of the order so that you can keep the consumer aware. This way, you can track shipments whenever you anticipate them to come longer than expected and easily fix issues.

5. Not Enough Brand Display.

Through dropshipping, it may be hard to guarantee the brand remains to be seen in the customer's overall experience. You may not want people to forget regarding you, so it's important to insert as many locations as possible into your brand. You should have customized packing slips, stickers and custom exterior packaging to hold the name included after delivery. Sending a follow-up thank you message or a survey to remind about of you and prove them you think for their feedback at the same time is also not a bad idea.

6. Return Complications.

If you do not have a system for returns set up, things can get messy very quickly. You and your vendor will have to establish a refund policy to avoid this. Customers are going to wait for their refund expectantly, and being disorganized on that front and will not make them feel good. They may also need guidelines explaining how or where to return the product. Organizing a structure for this will save a good amount of confusion and irritation for both you and the client.

7. Selling Trademarked Products

When most people learn about dropshipping and realize that it is not that complicated to do the process, they picture all the things they might sell and make a quick buck.

Many of these goods are items which have been trademarked by a manufacturer. Selling these goods without the manufacturer's specific consent to be a retail agent will lead you to legal issues. This can not only lead to the end of your online shop, but you can also be held personally responsible.

You should, consequently, look at generic items which you can add to your variety of products for sale. Best still, you should swap in goods with white marks. They are plain goods that are available to those who rebrand them through the manufacturer. You will order and get these items customized to suit the brand and display them.

8. Picking the Wrong Field

Once you have abandoned thoughts of selling any product you come across, by concentrating on one field, you can develop your dropshipping business.

You might, however, select the wrong niche in which to operate. Maybe you should pick a niche that isn't lucrative. This may be that it's out of vogue or it's simply not meant for shopping online.

Therefore, to see what will earn you money, you have to do proper market analysis. "Market research" might sound like a complex process in which only major brands participate.

Simple Google searches will, therefore, show you what individuals are interested in and where they purchase them.

9. Poor Relationship With Suppliers

Your vendors are part of your business; they promise that you have the best goods and that they supply your consumers with them. You can be inclined, though, to consider them as workers and handle them as though they are in the hierarchy on a lower rung.

They're not. They are your friends, without whom it would be effectively dead for your dropshipping business. Therefore, you can establish a better relationship with them.

This will have its benefits. When negotiating costs for commodity stock, a strong partnership will work in your favor.

10. Lowering Price To Extreme Levels

Reducing your prices to knock out your competition is also one of the dropshipping failures to avoid.

This is a logical way for you to rise your dropshipping business, you might think. You could have been no farther from the facts. Very low prices indicate to potential customers that your product may be of poor quality.

11. Poor Website Structure

The progress of your dropshipping company depends on the shopping experience your clients have when they browse your online store.

Thus, you have to make sure everything is convenient for them. However, you could rush through the process of establishing your website due to low barrier for entrance into dropshipping. Many beginners do not have the coding skills required to construct an online store.

In conclusion, the primary interest is the customer's experience. Although inventory management and shipping are not your responsibility, you can also ensure that all is well handled. All of these dropshipping failures can be prevented with adequate preparation and careful management, and the business can better manage.

Chapter 9. Smooth Running tips for Your Dropshipping Business

Well, you've done your research, decided to agree on the right dropship goods and roped in the right possible supplier. All of you are planned to begin dropshipping goods and make the mullah! Setting up the company, though, is typically one thing, but a totally different ball game is to manage it on a day-to-day basis. Even if it's a dropshipping company, there are various facets of running a business that you have to remember as a retailer: marketing, refunds, refunds, repairs, inventory, distribution, customer service, and far more. So dive into all these different aspects of managing a dropshipping business.

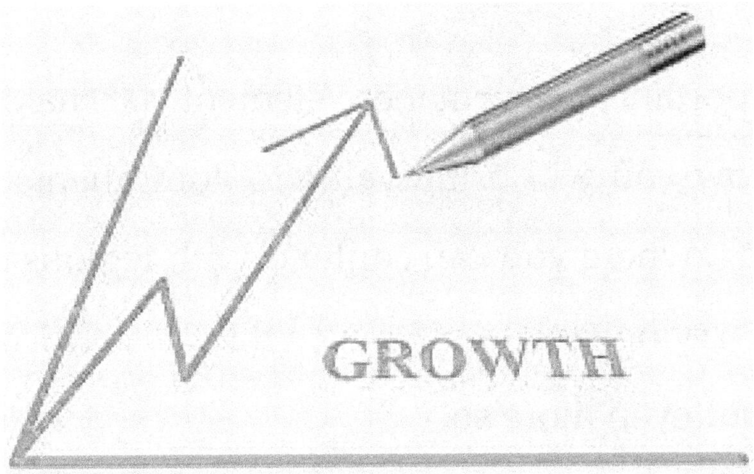

So far, when covered a lot of details, it involves everything from the fundamentals of dropshipping to the nuances of finding a niche and managing the business. You should have much of a base by now to begin investigating and establishing your own dropshipping company comfortably.

It's possible to get confused and lose track about what's really necessary, with too much to consider. That's why we've built this list of key elements for success. This are the main "must-do" acts that can make the new company or ruin it. If you can perform these effectively, you would be able to get a bunch of other stuff wrong and yet have a decent probability of success.

1. Add Value

The most important performance element is making a good roadmap on how you will bring value to your clients. In the field of dropshipping, where you can contend with legions of other "me too" stores carrying related items, this is critical for both corporations, but even more so.

With dropshipping, it's reasonable to think you're marketing a product to consumers. Yet good small merchants realize that they are offering insights, ideas and solutions, not just the commodity they deliver. You assume you're an e-commerce seller, but you're in the information industry as well.

If you can't create value by quality data and advice, price is the only thing you're left to contend on. While this has been an effective technique for Walmart, it will not help you grow a successful company for dropshipping.

2. Focus on SEO and marketing

The opportunity to push traffic to the new platform is a near second to providing value as a main key factor. A shortage of traffic to their sites is the #1 concern and annoyance faced by modern e-commerce retailers. So many retailers have been slaving away on the ideal platform for months just to unleash it into a community that has no clue it exists.

For the success of your company, advertising and driving traffic is completely necessary and challenging to outsource well, particularly if you have a limited budget and bootstrap your business. In order to build your own SEO, publicity, outreach and guest posting abilities, you have to consider taking the personal initiative.

Within the first 6 - 12 months, where no one know who you are, this is particularly crucial. You need to devote at least 75 percent of your time on publicity, SEO and traffic development for at least 4 to 6 months after your website launch, which is right, 4 to 6 months. You can start reducing and coast a little on the job you put in until you've built a strong marketing base. But it's difficult, early on, to bring so much emphasis on advertising.

3. Marketing Your Dropshipping Business

Marketing is indeed a subjective field, and that there are a billion strategies which can be used to position your brand successfully whilst driving awareness and sales of your brand. It will even help you root out the remainder of the market if the approach is well planned.

4. Social Media Source

Social networking is one of the most efficient ways to promote, advertise, attract clients and share content, so when social networks are now used for digital marketing, it comes as no surprise. For example, Facebook has more than 1.7 billion active members from diverse walks of life, and it is this diversity that makes it so appealing to online marketers.

One thing to note is that it's important to content. No matter how perfect a platform is or how good the product you are offering is, without high quality content backing it up, it means nothing.

5. Customer Ratings & Reviews

A few bad customer ratings will actually ruin a business in dropshipping business model. Think about it: As you order online from websites like ebay and aliexpress, the quality ranking and what other consumers had to tell about it will be one of the determining purchase variables, too, with decrease delivery. A few positive feedback will also give you an advantage over the competition because that is what will help you convert traffic to your website successfully.

6. Email Marketing

In a digital marketer's pack, this one of the most neglected tools. To keep your clients in the loop for any major changes within company, email marketing may be used: Price increases, promotions, coupons, content related to the commodity, and content unique to the industry are only some of the forms email marketing may be utilized.

7. Growth Hacking

Growth hacking is a cheap but highly productive way to get online creative marketing campaigns. A few definitions of growth hacking involve retargeting old campaigns and featuring in your own niche as a guest writer for a popular website. Any of this commonly involves content marketing.

Chapter 10. How To Maximize Your Chances Of Success?

There are only a couple more tips you should adopt to maximize the chances of long-term growth if you are willing to take the plunge and attempt dropshipping. Second, that doesn't mean you can approach a dropshipping business because it's risk-free simply because there are no setup costs involved with purchasing and managing goods. You're also spending a lot of time choosing the right dropshippers while designing your website, so consider it as an investment and do careful preliminary research.

1. Things To Remember

What do you want to sell? How profitable is the surroundings? How can you gain clients and distinguish yourself? Inside the same room, is there a smaller niche that is less competitive? When they find a particular market and curate their goods like a pro, most individuals who operate a purely dropshipping model have seen the most growth, ensuring that any last item they offer is a successful match for their niche audience with their brand.

After you develop your list of possible dropshippers, carry out test orders and then watch for the items to arrive, thinking like a consumer. How long can any order take? What is the feeling of unboxing like? What is the commodity standard itself? This will help you distinguish between possible dropshippers or confirm that positive consumer service is offered by the one you want.

Note that the goods themselves may not be the differentiator for your business.

After you have chosen your dropshippers and products, note that the products themselves may not be the differentiator for your business. So ask what else you should count on to make the deal.

This is another explanation why test orders are a wonderful idea since they encourage you to obtain the item and explain its functionality and advantages as a client might. In a way which really shows it off, you can even take high-quality, professional pictures of the product. Armed with exclusive explanations of the goods and images that are separate from all the other product photos, you would be able to start standing out.

Your bread and butter is definitely going to be a well-executed campaign strategy, so devote time and money on each section of it, from finding your potential audience to interacting with influencers on social media in your niche. Targeted commercials can be a perfect way to kick start your site to bring your name on the mind of your client base.

When it relates to your return policies, delivery contact and customer support, ensure your ducks are in a line. You'll need to do what you could to serve as the buffer between a dropshipper and your client if something goes wrong somewhere in the process. Understand the typical cost of return for each item so that you will notice whether it is large enough to denote a quality issue.

If you suspect a consistency problem, talk to your dropshipper or try a different supplier to your issues.

Eventually, note that dropshipping is not a model of "all or nothing." Many of the more profitable corporations follow a hybrid model, making or shipping in-house some goods and employing dropshippers to fill the gaps. The dropshippers are not the key profit-drivers for these firms but are instead a simple, inexpensive way to provide clients with the "extras" they can enjoy. Before you put it in-house, you can even use dropshipped products for upsells, impulse sales, or to try a new model.

As long as you consider the above tips to ensuring that the one you chose is suitable for your business needs, there is definitely a lot to learn from the streamlining and flexibility of using a dropshipper. You will make your dropshipping store run for you in no time with a little of research, negotiation, and setup!

Conclusion

So that concludes our definitive dropshipping guide. You now learn how to set up to kick start your new dropshipping business if you've made it here. Starting up your own business often involves a certain degree of dedication, effort, and ambition to make things work, much as in every other undertaking in life. It's not only about building the business but also about pushing through and knowing how to manage it on a daily basis.

The greatest feature of dropshipping is that you will practice in real-time by checking your goods and concepts, and all you have to do is drop it from your shop if anything doesn't work. This business concept is indeed a perfect opportunity for conventional business models to try out product concepts. Dropshipping creates a secure place to innovate to see what happens without incurring any substantial damages that will surely give business owners the courage to state that they have a working idea of how the market works. The dropshipping business model is an interesting business model to move into with little initial expense and relatively little risk.

A perfect choice to drop shipping if you are only starting to sell online and would like to test the waters first. It's a great way to start your business, even if the margins are low.

As dropshipping can still get started with little investment, before they build their market image, businessmen can start with that too. Ecommerce sites such as Ebay, Shopify, Alibaba and social networking, such as Instagram, Twitter, Reddit, provide vast expertise in user base and content marketing. It also helps newbies to know about establishing an online store, optimizing conversions, generating traffic and other basics of e-commerce.

That's what you need to learn about beginning a dropshipping. Just note, it's not the hard part to launch your dropshipping store, the real challenge is when you get trapped, and your stuff is not being sold. Do not panic, and keep checking as it happens. You're going to get a product soon that sells well.

Private Label Crash Course

Build Your First 6-Figure Business Supported by a Collection of 9+1 Profitable Strategies. Find the Best Products, Build an Enlighten Team and Start Your Personal Brand

By

Amir Lime

Table of Contents

Introduction

A private label is where a person or corporation paying another business to make a commodity without its name, emblem, etc. The person or business then applies to the packaging their name and design. So, what sorts of items should be labeled privately? From skincare and dietary treatments and infant essentials, pet products, and kitchen utensils, pretty much all under the sun. The benefit of private labeling is that nothing innovative needs to be produced or developed by you. You can add your mark on it as long as it's not a proprietary commodity and label it yours. For the last ten years, private labels have risen by at least double the number of popular household products. In reality, there is a lot of conversation about the rise of private labels or retail brands around the world these days. Or we need to claim private brands, maybe since they are indeed labels by the end of each day. Opportunities to have ever-better-value offerings for both of us as consumers. Possibilities for everyone to push the main factors transforming the world of today and tomorrow. Yes, it's not the Private Label curse. It could well, in truth, be a present. A blessing that pushes us all to question the status quo again. A gift that pushes one to step positively with some of the main big forces that form the world of today to collaborate together more successfully and collaboratively. A blessing that is increasingly important to all of us, whether in the United Kingdom, the United States, China, or Scandinavia. If we like it or not, Private Label will soon have a single category of quick products in the country. In the last ten years, private labels have risen at least double the amount of popular consumer packaged goods brands. How did the Private Label expand at the above remarkable pace, and what lessons does it give players in the more narrowly established markets of fast-moving consumer goods? We like to think of it as a food event, but it's increasingly a complete experience of consumption. Flavors' globalization, marketers, and individuals have made Private Label a global fact. More and more, Private Label is the face of today's retailer. Comprehend it. This isn't going to go away. Act about it. Perhaps we should name them PRIVATE Companies from now on. Perhaps we might create very different tactics to survive if we began naming them brands instead of labels. Brands are concerned about combating their closest competing brand. Will they behave as though their closest advertised rival is the Private Label? Maybe they could, because maybe if they did, they might behave very differently in reality. The commodity has gone on. In turn, as Private Label has become a brand power in its own right, it has become privatized. It cannot be ignored as a single mark anymore. It's something a ton more. While taken out of context, Private Label is turning controversial for this cause, maybe more than any other, placing owners on the backhand side and retail section on the offensive. Neither group appears especially keen to publicly address it or cooperate on something outside development. Products have brought copycatting stores to court, and dealers have de-listed popular brands from their racks. There's a tiny concession space. It increasingly distorts agreed shopping habits and usage trends in order to exacerbate problems more. It is a brand that can often account for two out of three physical transactions made by your consumer. A brand that is gradually seen as an alternate product and value of parity. A company that will out-weigh and out-image any typical brand by exploiting the retailer's corporate strength and spending. A brand that can drive producers into a vicious cycle of loss in the market. A trillion-dollar market that, as you realize its sheer scale and future effects, must be the least evaluated and poorly understood industry around. An industry that in the years to come is going to get a lot larger. There would theoretically be billions of dollars of sales redirected by brand owners to this power. Are you confident your plans are ready? The remedies? But, as the solution, what do people recommend? Lower costs, increase efficiency, and be more imaginative. This is not just a remedy that you can pursue as a standard component of your business growth. It is simply not sufficient. This is an opportunity that requires the unusual and the unconventional. Or else rise to the challenge. The Private Label is a wake-up call from a brand creator. Wake up to the truth in the company. Wake up in search of a shopper. Wake up to what you might theoretically do for your company. Wake up to proactivity for real. Wake up to a chance to get the rest of the planet back into communication with your company. Private label has arisen from the conventionally held assumption that firms will benefit and conquer the competition by providing either higher value at a higher cost for their consumers (or shoppers) or fair value at a cheaper cost (retailer brands). In other terms, it's a preference between distinction (or innovation) and low cost, and it's safe to assume that only then have retailers fallen into the former to offer the latter to the shopper reliably in spades. As Coke (and Tesco) can also inform you, it pays dividends to see the brand on any street corner. However, as some of our research highlights would demonstrate, there is still a significant perception difference between Private Label and existing manufacturer labels in terms of quality/value. As long as the shopper is concerned, at least, without the other, one will not thrive, and broadly speaking, maker labels are better positioned to offer sound 'innovation' and 'value' to retailers. Just 16% of shoppers in all regions sincerely agree that a supermarket of retailer-owned goods can only be expected in the future. So, we think there is a potential for brands to constantly reinvent themselves through shopper intuition, deeper brand commitment, and creativity. The potential for retailers to continuously add value is there. The potential exists for producers to maximize their manufacturing ability and for interactions to be reinvented by agencies. But most critically, the potential is there to constantly impress and entertain the shopper, far beyond all their hopes. The other alternative frequently provided is to get yourself into making a private label. However, you may be compelled by Private Label to analyze the very simple essence of the company in which you are and to doubt whether it is strong enough to move you further. Ask for your goods. Ask how and to whom you are offering. Ask if you still are tuning into the agents of transition. Your corporate purpose issues. Ask if you have the best staff and processes to meet this crucial problem. Finally, Private Label is a concern for manufacturers alike. Knowing how to profitably manage it without undermining the very essence of the organization you are with. And the manufacturers that you work with. Yes, you may assume that you can survive without them. Yet we're advising, be very, very patient. If you want to be a genuinely successful marketing tool in terms of bringing to the shopper, you need one another. In comparison, we exist in an age in which the newspapers are building up major global supermarket chains as the latest businesses to despise. Why are you stopping this? As the messenger, you use Private Label, a messenger that not only reveals that you deliver excellent value and costs but also indicates that you think for your consumer and their long-term social needs. And you are really doing what you can to support them. Now, even more on this. The private label is, to a great degree, a hidden force. The conservative nature of the subject-matter literature tends to downplay its actual place in the world, a function far from conservative in fact, and a role in which Private Label is undeniably the single greatest influence on our businesses and goods today. Brands, engagement professionals, and scholars have consistently ignored or underestimated this. That's got to change.

Chapter 1: Getting Started-Private Label

A private label is where a person or corporation paying another business to make a commodity without its name, emblem, etc. The person or business then applies to the packaging their name and design. So, what sorts of items should be labeled privately? From skincare and dietary treatments and infant essentials, pet products, and kitchen utensils, pretty much all under the sun. The benefit of private labeling is that nothing innovative needs to be produced or developed by you. You can add your mark on it as long as it's not a proprietary commodity and label it yours. A private label product is made and marketed under a retailer's brand name through a contract or third-party maker. You specify all about the commodity as the distributor-what goes into it, how everything is packaged, what the logo looks like-you pay to get it manufactured and shipped to your shop. This is in relation to purchasing goods with their corporate logos on them from other businesses. A successful brand identity can be the crucial base for building loyal customers, customer growth, and a competitive edge. Care of your corporate name as your company's face is how you are viewed by the audience. Without a detailed, excellently defined brand identity, the consumer might not realize who you are. In the end, you need to create a personal link. The potential exists for producers to maximize their manufacturing ability and for interactions to be reinvented by agencies. But most critically, the potential is there to constantly impress and entertain the shopper, far beyond all their hopes. The other alternative frequently provided is to get yourself into making a private label. However, you may be compelled by Private Label to analyze the very simple essence of the company in which you are and to doubt whether it is strong enough to move you further.

1.1 What is Private Label?

A private label product is made and marketed under a retailer's brand name through a contract or third-party maker. You specify all about the commodity as the distributor-what goes into it, how everything is packaged, what the logo looks like-you pay to get it manufactured and shipped to your shop. This is in relation to purchasing goods with their corporate logos on them from other businesses.

1.2 Private Label Categories

Almost every consumer product category has both branded and private label offerings, including:

- Condiments and salad dressings
- Cosmetics
- Personal care
- Frozen foods
- Dairy items
- Beverages
- Household cleaners
- Paper products

1.3 Different types of Private Label as profitable strategies

Generic Private Label

Generic private-label goods are one of the conventional private label tactics used to provide the price-conscious consumer with a low-price alternative. The brand doesn't matter to these consumers. With limited advertising and no marketing, the goods are inexpensive, undifferentiated, poor inconsistency. In commoditized and low-involvement goods, these private labels are primarily present. For both discount stores in Western nations, this technique is widespread.

Copycat Brands

In order to draw buyers, manufacturers play on the price point, retaining the packaging identical to a national brand that offers a sense of the product's similar consistency. These goods are reverse engineered, utilizing factories of identical technologies from national brand products. In wide categories that have a clear market champion, certain private labels are mostly present. In the detergent group, Massive Corporation blindly embraces the copycat brand approach. Detergents against rival products with identical packaging have been launched, albeit at a cheaper price.

Premium store brands

Retailers now have started utilizing private labels, rather than just as a pricing strategy, as a store point of difference. Premium store brands are valued higher and are also high in performance than the national brands. Here, the customer proposal is to be the greatest brand that money will purchase. In the retailer's shop, these products get influential eye-catching locations. In the advertising, the manufacturer insists on the excellent consistency of the goods.

Value innovators

Retailers manufacture goods that have all the value-adding characteristics and eliminate the non-value-adding characteristics in order to reduce costs, one point ahead of the copycat approach, and thus provide the customer with the best value deal. The danger of being imitated also rests in these labels. As it produces furniture under a modern market paradigm that involves self-service, assembling, and transporting yourself, Ikea is renowned for its better goods.

1.4 White Label vs. Private Label Dropshipping?

You can select between white label and private label dropshipping if you want to launch an online store. Both words define goods that have been branded by a reseller, but the two definitions very distinctly. Particularly to beginners, they may seem quite complicated, so let's go through each one and explain their relative benefits.

Private Labeling

Private marking is where a company selectively makes a commodity for a store that offers it under its own name. Costco utilizes private marking, for instance, by marketing its own "Kirkland" brand that no other store can offer. As a consequence, goods with private labels are typically less pricey than national brands. Plus, they can be very lucrative if they're promoted properly. Dropshipping is a convenient method for private-label goods to be distributed. You will find a dropshipping provider if you are an online shop owner who can offer items directly to you and incorporate your branding. Dropshipping is an e-commerce market concept in which no inventory is held by the manufacturer. The retailer, instead, manages the packaging, packing, and delivery of goods to the end customer. In other terms, for dropshipping, the goods are delivered directly to consumers, and they are never used by stores.

White Labeling

A white-label product is a manufactured product that a company makes but is rebranded by marketers to make it look as though it had been produced. Each dealer is authorized to resell the item under its own title and labeling. Unlike private labels, several retailers may market a white-label commodity. For e.g., you can have your own branding and labels on the goods that are delivered if you wish to market a product under your brand name utilizing the dropshipping business strategy. It is often safer to search at something that already has a market when it comes to items with a white mark. It's dangerous to produce goods with white marks that consumers are not comfortable with. It's safer to go for existing brands that people regularly use. As with private labels, dropshipping makes it simple to market online white-label goods. Again, the items are delivered directly from the producers to customers, and the commodities are seldom seen by dealers.

Advantages & Disadvantages of White Labeling

You won't have to go through the complicated logistics of making a commodity in one of these two e-commerce market models. You can save a lot of time and money without significant expenditure of time and energy in product design and production. In essence, you will concentrate on selling the commodity to the target group and branding it. In order to expand your company, you won't spread yourself thin and can concentrate on other areas of expertise. So, let's go through the common advantages and disadvantages of each business model:

Advantages of White Labeling

There are some real benefits of the white labeling market model, including:

- **It saves time and money.**

It's just cheaper to white mark an established commodity instead of wasting resources on developing a product from scratch.

- **Gain a large profit**

In general, white label goods are exclusively marketed by suppliers and may be bought at cheap market rates.

Disadvantages of White Labeling

There are, on the other side, some risks of white marking, including:

- **Limited options for branding**

Because it will be the producer or retailer who makes the white label product's bottle, label, and packaging, depending on the concept, you can just decide what it will deliver for you.

- **Limited choices of products**

Just the goods that the maker produces will be preferred, and you will not be allowed to produce anything special to the market.

- **Competition is tough**

It is challenging to stand out from the other online vendors that, white-label or not, sell the same items.

1.5 Dropshipping Private Label

We have addressed that different dropshipping products are among the simplest methods for private or white label items to be distributed. So, let's go about how private or white label items can be dropshipped.

Finding a supplier

In order to achieve the sustainability of online shops, having a successful dropshipping supplier is utterly crucial. In quest of finding a directory of dropshipping vendors who sell private label facilities, you should look at business websites or just do a search on Google. Seeking a niche will allow you and your business to stand out from other retail vendors. Make sure that you conduct consumer analysis to figure out what sort of thing you would prefer to rebrand or distribute.

Establishing the identity with the brand

A successful brand identity can be the crucial base for building loyal customers, customer growth, and a competitive edge. Care of your corporate name as your company's face is how you are viewed by the audience. Without a detailed, excellently defined brand identity, the consumer might not realize who you are. In the end, you need to create a personal link. Brand awareness must be expressed in the products, slogan, website, and packaging. It can offer a' derived from human attributes' to your brand. Brands with a very well-established personality make the brand intimately relatable, connecting consumers at a relational level and having to have the commodity in their lives. This is relevant for dropshipping products, including the private and white labels.

Increase awareness about your label and brand

Growing your brand recognition is another important move towards building a profitable brand. If the product is fresh, then identifying your target customers and discovering ways to draw consumers to your shop is the very first thing you'll want to achieve. This is so if it's the private label dropshipping goods. Here are some forms that brand recognition can be improved without any expense:

- Build content on your website with the addition of a blog
- Developing your social network online identity
- To engage and network with more clients and get product feedback.
- To maximize your keyword scores, perform SEO.

1.6 Deciding What to Private Label

You might be wondering about what's a competitive commodity to private label. The secret to this phase and probably the most crucial step in beginning a private label company is researching and putting efforts into finding a good product. You ought to figure out which products/services are in the market to ensure if your product would sell. To see what people, look for on the internet and get ideas about what you can offer from there, you can use programs available online. If you intend to launch your private label company on online marketplaces, you'll want to use a testing method that actually monitors what individuals are searching for on that platform. For this, popular programs include

Helium 10 and Jungle Scout. They both provide several resources to help you continue your market path with your private label.

What Makes A Good Private Label Product?

The biggest point to hold in mind when applying for a private label for a commodity is to find one that:

It is in strong market demand and has limited competition from sellers.

This can help you stop being trapped with things that you will not offer.

Has a strong margin for benefit

Taking into consideration how much the item would cost you vs. how much you will market it for. If the item is held in a warehouse, plus the expenses involved with sale online, don't neglect to take into account the delivery costs from your source to you and from you to your client, packing and storage fees.

If you can manage the expenses

If you have a $1,000 or $10,000 startup investment budget, you need to take into consideration how many units you will need/want to buy and how much of the budget you will spend.

How to Find Suppliers

It's time to search for a producer or trade firm that provides private label service once you have a commodity in mind that you would like to private label. You can select anywhere in the world to make your goods. And several times, the type of service/product you select would rely on where you choose to get your product made. For e.g., China might be worth considering if you are trying to sell toys or gadgets because they seem to produce a ton of these types of items at very low prices. Consider looking for Alibaba or AliExpress if you want to go on this path. Both of these platforms are bulk markets where the goods are identified by suppliers and trade houses, where you can find almost everything. Because with all our federal rules, it's a great choice to source in the U.S. whether you want to offer food, dietary foods, cosmetic goods, or something else you bring in or on your body. Check on Google for items sourced domestically. Say you're searching for vegan deodorant source, just type in Google "vegan perfume private label

U.K." to get a list of companies that can use vegan deodorants for private label.

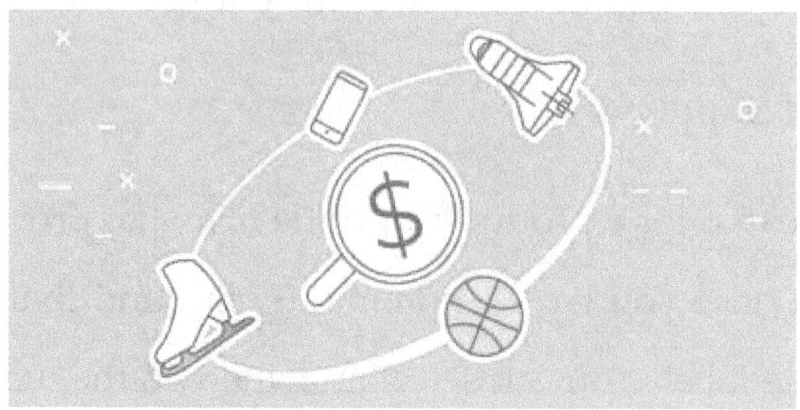

What to Ask Private Label Suppliers

Once you've drawn up a list of possible vendors, calling each one and posing some questions is a smart idea.

Pricing Per Unit

The price would usually already be accessible for you to see on the website for each item. However, depending on how many units you order, most manufacturers give a discount. Knowing this data would also assist you in estimating the gross margin.

MOQ

In the private label/wholesale environment, this is a generic word used because it stands for "minimum order" or the minimum number of units you will order at a time. On their website/product listing, most vendors will mention their MOQ, although you will only have to inquire for some. The MOQ of a producer can be as few as five units, although it can be 1,000 and beyond for some. Although this may be negotiable often, asking this upfront is a smart move so that you can prepare and budget appropriately.

Customization

It is nice to know what the factory is and will not do in advance so that you can stop trying to swap vendors later unless you are seeking to apply your branding to the package, customize packages, or make modifications to the product.

Production Time

It is helpful to know how long it would take your provider to meet orders when your private label company continues to expand, and you continue to prepare for potential orders. Typically, the norm is around 15 days (depending on the commodity and order size), so it can go up from there.

Response Time

Take notice of how long it takes for the supplier to get back to you, bearing in mind that you are initiating a long-term future trading partnership. You would want to make sure that your communication individual is trustworthy, prompt, and specifically addresses your questions. If your provider is based in another country, take into consideration that they are in a separate time zone and that you will not automatically obtain a reply. During their business hours, being present will allow the operation easier.

Samples

Ask for prototypes such that the consistency and particular requirements can be measured. Many vendors can submit a sample free of charge, while others may start charging a small fee. Anyway, it's certainly not something you'd skimp on, especially if you're trying to give the highest service to your customers.

Customizing Your Product

In how your product can market, customizing your product will play a huge role. Question yourself, "What's going to set my version apart from the competition?" The response to this is key in having a prospective customer select your product over the product of a more known, well-reviewed business. Perhaps it's as quick as providing color combinations or getting fancy packaging, or it might be easier to enhance a function that you want more in-depth. Such customizations, such as packaging upgrades, are likely to be achieved by your supplier, and some can be accomplished through yourself or by your suppliers, such as custom marking with product specifics and a logo. Customizing the goods in any form is the main message here. Stand out by having it different (and better) than the rivals '. By basically slapping the mark on it, you don't want to sell the same exact thing as another brand.

You are selling your Private Label product.

You may pick anywhere to market your private-label line of items. Here's an extensive list of online sales places or suggestions on how to get into shops.

A Personal Online Store

Such customizations, such as packaging upgrades, are likely to be achieved by your supplier, and some can be accomplished through yourself or by your suppliers, such as custom marking with product specifics and a logo. Customizing the goods in any form is the main message here. Stand out by having it different (and better) than the rivals '. By simply yanking your tag on it, you wouldn't want to give the same product as yet another brand.

Brick-And-Mortar

Sitting the goods on the shelf of a physical shop offers consumers the ability to see your product that they would never have dreamed of it otherwise. In other words, customers have to practically "search" for services or products they want to buy online. But if they don't think about it, they're not going to search and probably won't find it unless you pay serious bucks promoting it. If shoppers are still in a shop and happen to see it, it builds brand/product recognition at least. Fees and requirements for getting shelf-space vary by store, but it can be a decent place to start from local, family-owned stores. Read more regarding boutique collaborations or having your own storefront.

Markets

Markers and art fairs for producers are on the increase. Consumers love to shop locally and want to help their community's artisans. They're a perfect way to get instant input from customers, too. Find out how to start trading and find craft markets at farmer's markets.

Don't limit yourself.

Start with a variety of channels, in-person shops, and websites. You would be able to see over a span of time how many sales you create from each one, how much money each produces, etc. You should just stick doing what's profitable, then. It is certainly a road to launch your private label company, and it will be months until you can bring the goods on the market. But the trip can be well worth it if you do your product testing, pick the best source, separate the product from the market, and price it right.

Chapter 2: Profitable Strategies in Building Six-Figure Business

For private-label products, manufacturers may raise gross margins by managing the whole supply chain from manufacture to distribution. Clothing traders have been pushing different private-label options for years. Costco has the Kirkland private-label name. Nordstrom's got Caslon. And Kohl's has Sonoma as its in-house, billion-dollar brand. Although online stores have supplied other industries with private label labels, basic products for tangible products focused on low-cost hardware and office equipment, the move to clothes implies a brazen policy expansion. Any volume seller is looking at the advantages of growing private-label brand's goods in order to drive sustainability and connect with a more aware and conscious millennial generation who are known for not being very brand loyal.

2.1 Private Label for Profitability

Profits are powered by private labels. A private-labeled commodity or product with parity in operation and consistency with major labels will cost manufacturers 40 to 50 percent less to develop and sell to consumers. In order to negotiate with online marketplace empires and other online suppliers who offer low-cost products without caring about reducing margins, merchants will then switch around to provide greater discounts. Online, where customers have 100 percent pricing transparency, this is especially essential. This functions on both luxury and commodity items. Building and maintaining a private label often enables manufacturers to develop exclusive goods for higher prices or to manufacture commodity products below brands at a sustainable price. To boost their inventory rotation, manufacturers are now using private-label tactics. Retail stores with services from private labels could also have more than four seasons a year. An innovative team in private label, such as the JCPenney team of 250 designers working in-house or the internal production and procurement departments of Nordstrom, will contend on an equal footing with fast-trending fashion stores like H&M.

Factors to be Considered

It may be dangerous to hop into this business without carefully thinking it over. Before investing and dedicating time to a privately-label approach, here are some factors to be considered:

- **Identifying low cost and high-quality manufacturer**

A colossal advantage is strong production suppliers, while poor manufacturers or suppliers are a horrific liability. Spend the effort to do it correctly. There are hundreds or thousands of suppliers capable of producing stuff that you would need. Find the producer that fits all the requirements for price and consistency; often, identifying the markets that are relevant. You may also want to learn from Portugal or Vietnam for clothing. Vietnam, South Korea, and China have manufacturing expertise in electronics. Take note that costs for suppliers differ greatly depending on the order's size.

- **Strengthen the Skills in Design and Procurement**

The private label includes relationships with producers of agricultural and consumer goods, component retailers, multinational warehouses, and distribution suppliers. Will you broaden the current partnerships between suppliers? If not, determine whether to consult the staff or purchase the expertise that will render the retail company a key competency of the strategy regarding the private label. Consider a completely dedicated bet on vertical trading, too.

- **Using brand pricing and external signs as guiding principles for pricing policy**

Research your rival brands closely while designing your own products under the banner of a private label. Retailers ought to make up their mind whether to generate the product as a luxury product and expend marketing expenses or to position it as an alternate brand by selling below national labels. If product attributes can be readily contrasted and placed as a substitute brand, it is important to consider the price point of comparable goods to position them correctly against competitors' national brand/products label brands. In other situations, were comparing features is not something very straightforward. Retailers can use a number of internal market pointers for pricing, such as site traffic, ratings, consumer feedback, and retailers can recognize the popularity of the product. Today, if a commodity is popular/interest-generating, but the converging performance is low, this can cause a price reduction/promotion intervention.

- **Acknowledge the differences in categories and manage them smartly**

Consumers can browse for functionality within a particular perceived cost sub-set for white and hard goods. Buyers searching for features are opting for a dryer or washing machine. Potential customers are looking for other qualities, such as cloth, shape, trendiness, for soft items like clothing. Those features deter similarities.

- **Decide Efficient Customized Label Blend**

The best combination of private label and branded items has to be determined by retailers. Are buyers looking for a feature in a certain product category or range on the website? Collecting web search data can help marketers make a choice. They have to remember the client base as well. If the consumer pool is predominantly 28- to 51-year-old buyers, private label goods can be more value aware and prefer small-scale proliferation.

- **Implement Algorithmic, Data-Driving Pricing Methods**

With constantly evolving customer preferences, at every given level in time, you should be able to recognize demand levels and continually seek the optimum price value. Factor in leveraging algorithms based on technology systems to easily evaluate price levels and strategies; when priced carefully with supporting data, private-label brands also deliver unexpected revenues. For e.g., the commodity was priced well below the national brand by a generic manufacturer of merchandise with a very well private label refrigerator brand, just to experience a drop in revenue. The store began checking multiple price ranges, steadily pushing up the segment. Sales started to fall with the first $200 onwards. And, magically, revenue and traffic boomed until the price reached a hidden barrier. This sounds counterintuitive, but the private-label company has already been put in a competitive area with national labels in the view of the consumer. Instead of seeing it as a lower quality commodity, clients began to see it as domestic brands.

They were prepared to move since the price levels were always cheaper than domestic brands. In a considerably more profitable buyer zone, it was repositioned by moving the idea up the continuum. If consumers interpret things the same way with analytic pricing, the same SKU will gain double the profits. These are some of the most important elements in successfully initiating your private label initiative at any major retailer. Going over these basics will strip the efforts of the bulk of danger.

2.2 9+1 Pricing Strategies

Want to maximize profit on your product sales?

Aside from other publicity and business tactics, a strong pricing policy is indeed something you need to concentrate on. When setting the price for your goods or services, what considerations do you consider? When determining the prices for your goods or services, there are a number of considerations, including:

- Production cost
- positioning strategies
- competitor's products

- Distribution cost
- Target consumer base

When buying a commodity, price is a very important consideration for a buyer. A productive pricing system can also have a profound influence on the company's performance. And often, it decides whether or not the organization can succeed. So, what are those tactics you should suggest in order to improve the revenue and be more profitable?

Premium Pricing

Marketers put rates higher than their competitors or rivals for this promotional policy. However, it is used where there is a major competitive edge, and a relatively cheaper price is safe for the marketer or the organization to charge. For small businesses that offer exclusive services or products, high pricing is perfect. A corporation, however, can check that the packaging of the goods, its promotional campaigns, and the décor or luxury facilities of the store all fit to maintain the fixed price.

- **Example of Premium Pricing**

Let's take the example of luxury specialty retail stores that charge you a little extra but sell you exclusive styles and tailored clothing.

Penetration Pricing

To try to draw buyers? Ok, this technique is going to help you with the purpose. Lower rates are given on utilities or goods under this strategy. Although this technique is used by many emerging firms, it does appear to lead to an initial reduction of profits for the business. Over time, though, the growth of product or service recognition will drive revenues and allow small businesses to stand out. In the long run, as a business succeeds in entering the sector, its costs always end up growing to represent the condition of its role in the sector.

Economy Pricing

The advertisement expense of a service or commodity is held at a low in this strategy. The technique is used during a certain period where the organization does not invest much in promoting the service or product.

Example of Economy Pricing

The first few budget airlines, for instance, are offered at low rates in discount airlines to fill in the jet. A broad variety of businesses, from discount stores and generic grocery manufacturers, use Economy Pricing. The technique, though, maybe dangerous for small firms when they lack the market scale of larger corporations. Small companies can fail to make a sufficient profit with low rates, but strategically tailoring price-cuts to your most loyal customers or consumers may be a successful way to guarantee their loyalty for years to come.

Price Skimming

This technique is meant to assist enterprises in focusing on the sale of innovative services or goods. During the preliminary process, this strategy means setting high prices. The rates are then reduced steadily when the competitor's goods or services arrive on the market. When the product is first released in the marketplace, this price approach produces an image of exclusivity and good quality.

Psychology Pricing

This method of pricing deals with a client's psychology. For e.g., setting the price of a ring at $99 is likely to draw more clients than setting prices at $100. But the concern is, in terms of a very limited gap, why are consumers more drawn to a product's former price? Psychology suggests that on a price tag, customers prefer to give greater attention to the first digits. When stores apply $0.99 on product tags of $1.99 or $2.99, you can find identical promotional strategies. The purpose of this approach, therefore, is to build an image of greater value for the consumer.

Bundle Pricing

How often have you been persuaded to purchase a multipack of 6 packets for $2.99 instead of purchasing one packet for $0.65? Or an SMS kit instead of texting on the individual rates? Without sacrificing efficiency, we all enjoy commodities that cost us less. This is why package selling is a success for both the vendor and the consumer and is profitable. The vendor gets to sell more of their inventory, and for less cost, the consumer gets to purchase the product in bulk. For instance, if bundle package of chips is for $1.30 and 3 multipacks for2.50$. The probability of purchasing three packs is more than purchasing only one. Bundle pricing enhances the worth sense when you are actually offering your consumers anything for free.

Value Pricing

This technique is used when external forces such as increased rivalry or unemployment cause corporations to offer valuable promotional offerings or goods, e.g., combo offers or value meals at KFC and other restaurants, to sustain sales. Quality pricing lets a buyer know like for the same price, they are receiving a ton of product. In several respects, profit pricing is analogous to economic pricing. So, let's make this very clear that there is added benefit with regard to service or product in value pricing. Generally speaking, price cuts should not rise in value.

Promotional Pricing

Promotional pricing is a really common method for sales and can be used in different department stores and restaurants, etc. Part of this promotional policy are methods such as money off coupons, Buy One Get One Free, and promotions.

Cost-based Pricing

This method entails determining cost-based rates for the commodity to be made, shipped, and sold. In addition, a fair rate of profit is usually added by the corporation or sector to compensate for the risks as well as initiatives. Businesses such as Walmart and Ryanair are seeking to become low-cost suppliers. These businesses may set lower rates by constantly lowering costs whenever feasible. This undoubtedly contributes to lower profits but better profits and revenues. Companies with higher costs can, therefore, often rely on this approach to pricing. Yet, in general, in order to demand greater profits and rates, these businesses purposely generate higher costs. The aforementioned techniques are the most widely adopted strategies used by corporations to increase profit from sales of their product or service. In its own unique way, any pricing strategy is effective. Therefore, consider your marketplace and other conditions before selecting a pricing plan for your good or service to bring the most out of the strategy used. Therefore, becoming mindful of the competitive place when setting a price is important. What the clients or buyers anticipate in terms of the price should be considered in the marketing mix.

2.3 Best Practices in Private Label Branding

Can you recall when generic or non-national branded items with large black lettering and bad product consistency indicated simple white or yellow packing materials? After the unmemorable early days of supermarket labels, stores have clearly come a long way. In fact, many private label labels today are practically indistinguishable from their producer-branded equivalents on the shelves.

Align with and support the master (retail) brand

It is certainly no accident that some of the best private label company portfolios are those that tend to be in tune with the supermarket master brand's positioning and strategic purpose. Preferably, their positioning is strongly complementary to the supermarket master brand, enhancing the latter's equity and beneficial relationships.

Bring differentiation to the category; fulfill unmet customer needs.

When their products are additive to the supermarket, or better still, the overall competition, private label labels are maybe at their strongest. One way to achieve this is to bring the category to something completely differentiated. Another similar approach is to resolve consumer expectations that are not fulfilled by the big national labels. Importantly, this difference can be more than just a cheaper price than the brands of the manufacturer. In the good or service offering itself, private label labels can often be exclusive. Safeway is a perfect illustration of introducing distinction to the market and thereby addressing an increasingly unmet desire of the customer. Finally, creativity is another form in which private label labels may offer category and consumer distinction.

Establish clear boundaries for private label brands

There is also a temptation to expand it everywhere and anywhere in the shop once retailers effectively establish a good private label brand. This extends horizontally across types of goods and vertically across ranges of price/value. However, the tendency to over-extend or dilute the private label brand properties is resisted by better practice retailers.

Define brands based on emotional attributes

Since they feel an intrinsic bond to them, customers prefer to gravitate towards (and stay faithful to) products. There is no more for products with private labels than for brands with national suppliers. For private label labels, it is important that they stand for something more than just price/value and much more than a commodity attribute. They need to have an emotional advantage to which customers may connect. This essential nuance is understood by marketers that have become popular with exclusive labels and find ways to distill emotional equity through their private label brands.

Distinguish brands with a distinct identity and appropriate brand linkages

Finally, a distinctive and highly identifiable visual identity is established by leading label labels and embraces a clear messaging approach. They still maintain clear rules specifying the degree to which the private label mark may and should be identifiably affiliated with the supermarket master brand. An attractive visual presence and strategically advantageous brand design are undeniably part of what makes private label companies popular or leads to their downfall if overlooked.

2.4 Positives and Negatives of Private Label

Advantages

There is a legitimate explanation for retailers that are involved in flooding their stores with items with their brand name. Many of the main benefits of goods with private labeling include:

- **Handling Production**

Third-party suppliers operate at the behest of the supplier, providing full influence over the ingredients and consistency of the goods.

- **Control overpricing**

Retailers may also assess sales cost and efficient selling due to leverage over the product.

- **Adaptability**

In reaction to growing consumer demand for a new feature, smaller stores have the opportunity to move rapidly to bring a private label product into development, whereas larger firms might not be involved in a product or niche category.

- **Managing branding Decisions**

The company name and package concept produced by the manufacturer carry private label items.

- **Managing profitability**

Retailers monitor the amount of profitability their goods offer due to control over manufacturing expenses and pricing.

- **Increased margins**

Private labels enable manufacturers to sell and raise the profit margin more competitively on their goods. Compared to producing brands, several manufacturers gain 25-30 percent higher profit profits on private labels.

- **Customer loyalty**

Nowadays, consumers want goods manufactured locally, and they would like more if they enjoy the private label products. You would be the only outlet who would be willing to supply them with such goods. It is challenging to win the trust of individuals in the retail sector.

Disadvantages

As much as you have the financial capital to spend in creating such a commodity, the risks of introducing a private label brand are few. Primary drawbacks include:

- **Manufacturer dependency**

Since the manufacturing of your product range is in possession of a third-party vendor, working with accomplished businesses is critical. Otherwise, if the manufacturer gets into challenges, you might lose out on opportunities.

- **Difficulty building loyalty**

In a number of retail stores, existing household brands have the upper hand and can always be found. Only in your shops can your goods be sold, restricting consumer access to it. Restricted supply, of note, may also be an asset, providing clients an incentive to come back and purchase from you. Although private label goods are usually offered at a lower price point than their brothers of the corporate name, certain private label brands are also branded as luxury products, with a higher price tag to show it.

2.5 Keys to Private Label Greatness

As of late, we are doing a lot of innovative work in the Private Label sector, and here is a good refresher of The Core Values that we believe in for developing our own labels that are strategically convincing. We also see that there are particular fundamental stories in their creation throughout all great store brand cases, but there are seven values that they must abide by to be genuinely strategically convincing.

Principles of Equity and Environment

From a branding and design point of view, there has never been more interest in the grocery store and how we connect, affect purchasing decisions, and even construct theatre inside it. This is real in every part of the world. Of course, there is a reverence we all have to have for the cultural uniqueness of the grocery store, from country to country, since some customers are in the store just once a week, to other food and market experience where customers connect every day. Even with these diverse regional variations in frequency, familiarity, and satisfaction inside the retail shop, there is a common emphasis on making the store brand function more credibly and more convincingly with consumers in general.

The equity connection

Immersing oneself in the retailer's overarching goal, its perception and equity distinction as it is now, and what is achievable in the future is important. To achieve this, the right branding collaborators coordinate with the senior brass of the distributors with which they operate, as well as the organization's top merchants and store name specialists. They take into account all the main targets for which a merchant is fishing and then see how to enhance store brands as being one of the key tools to accomplish their task. Store products strengthen the retailer's total equity and vice-versa, and they struggle because they do not.

Environmental support

A kit can only do too many. Your store brand will get overloaded if it does not have the off-shelf environmental help in the vast stream of 40,000+ items that many of the largest supermarkets carry today. Beyond the box, give it existence and speech. To help your brand, use the theatre in the shop.

Be preferential

For supermarket brands, own products, exclusive brands, and the like, there are loads of common nomenclatures. "But whatever the language, don't treat your store brands to the larger national brands as weaker "stepchildren. Don't be afraid to handle your supermarket labels preferentially in the store, beyond the incisive box template for your company. In their importance, in their distribution of space, in their positioning of shelves, and in their show and cross-merchandising all throughout the shop. No need to apologize to the CPGs or succumb to the study of planograms.

Don't blindly follow.

For years, there has been a "follow the herd" attitude of store labels, and today it still persists. Because of what Walmart has achieved with Such Prices, many retailers we talk to now are terrified of "white" packaging. So often, individuals are hyper-attentive to the competition and norms and what's going around the market of store labels. The bottom line is that you can build your own vision in a very creative and special way. Do not blindly obey the naming conventions, color conventions, or typically mundane price-centered store brands set by broad categories and how they have traditionally behaved in order to reconsider anything intelligently.

Three layers have to work together.

Make sure you are not concerned with visual language alone with the positioning of the store labels and how they are to be fully distinguished for the future. This is the responsibility of a number of production agencies, who feel they are only employed to rewrite the store brand's aesthetic vocabulary. If we want to encourage these products to be produced differently, we need to understand how the graphic language is created, indeed, but also how it is structurally packaged and the language we use to orally convey the item. Graphic, systemic, and verbal languages all cohesively operate together.

Steve Jobs never asked the consumer.

Apple is one of the world's most creative and well-thought-out, profitable enterprises. When questioned what Steve Jobs felt about research in a New York Times report and how Apple uses it to direct new product creation, he replied, "None... it's not the job of consumers to know what they want." There are so many retailers that use research to store products in their innovative development phase, and this is a mistake. Customers will still turn to the protection and what is comfortable with them, but if they are the only sounding board, you will not have the most creative performance.

On the brand's positioning

In using the name of the shop on the individual store brand packaging, there are no universal guidelines, just as there are no generalizations to create about how large the store brand should stretch. Both of these brands had a very definitive strategic positioning when producing Greenway, Hartford Reserve, and Via Roma for A&P, and this relationship that established the role of the company was a very significant part of the process. Clearly describe it, know that you want to distinguish the brand rather than sheer costs, own it thoroughly in the consumer's head, and correctly reiterate it. In the development of an ambitious store brand platform, these ideals would suit you well because they are standards that the best supermarket brands live by with true conviction. The name brand industry continues to be guided by continuing innovative creativity, a true steel hand in spreading out from the single "price" veil, and to be persuasive in their own right. And store brands need to be promoted with vigor, motivation, and media support.

Chapter 3: Finding the Products & Starting Your Personal Brand

You should concentrate on creating a reputation before you start your company, one that is recognizable and valued, and a private label benefits both you and the retailer or supplier you select. The first move with your organization is importing the goods you choose to market, products that do not crack easily, which have satisfaction for the customer. The second and most significant move is to make your brand known to current and future clients. The more customers remember your brand, the higher it is possible that your revenue rate will be. Through selecting producers or suppliers who will submit your goods via Private Label, you will help this along. This operates by encouraging the consumer to position their orders with you, then deliver them to the retailer and directly dispatching the product. The return home address would be that of the company in most situations, but for Private Label, this will be yours. This ensures that whether they have any concerns or queries, the consumer would assume that the service/product has come from you, and they will only contact you. This helps you build up a brand reputation, but using trustworthy vendors, depends on you, and you deliver top-quality customer support. In general, manufacturers are willing to use private labels since it suggests that they do not have to be interested in any consumer problems. To sum up, while you are looking to get your brand out and develop a company without leeching on mainstream online market place/websites' popularity, a private label makes perfect sense. It will require a bit extra time to select a supplier since you must do the job yourself and guarantee that you work for the right supplier. Still, you will also gain a better profit when you take responsibility for the client support and are willing to negotiate the supplier's rates. A private label is where a person or corporation paying another business to make a commodity without its name, emblem, etc. The person or business then applies to the packaging their name and design. So, what sorts of items should be labeled privately? From skincare and dietary treatments and infant essentials, pet products, and kitchen utensils, pretty much all under the sun. The benefit of private labeling is that nothing innovative needs to be produced or developed by you. You can add your mark on it as long as it's not a proprietary commodity and label it yours.

3.1 How to Start Your Private Label Brand from Scratch?

Because of its profitability and consumer benefits, private labeling has boomed in prominence in recent years. To distinguish between larger vendors, more and more sellers create their products on and off e-commerce marketplaces. With 50 percent of one of the online markets, private labeling vendors, the rivalry is fierce. You need to realize what you're doing if you want to excel. To start a strong private label, you need the know-how, expertise, and money. When you place your logo and name on a standardized commodity, private labeling is. This separates the brand from related rivals and retailers. You have full power over your brand, with a private label. You establish a distinctive identity that is essential for successful promotion and the acquisition of consumers. Customers, not goods, are faithful to labels. Customer satisfaction and repeat business may be created through the private label. In the market, you still have the power of your price and place. A private label on the online marketplace enables you to build a different collection of items only for your product. This gives real estate devoted to your brand and assures that you are not vying against other retailers for the Buy Box. Since they get higher value, clients love private labels. Private-label goods are usually cheaper, but major stores' efficiency is the same, if not higher. In reality, at least one form of private label product is purchased by approximately 98 percent of customers. Depending on their lifestyle, customers may even buy goods. One study showed that clients prefer private labels for the price and choose them based on expertise. They buy from private labels that they most associate with. Ultimately, in a sea of rivals, a private label separates the name, allows you greater leverage over your revenues, and appeals to a niche client target. So, you have agreed to launch a private label of your own. The measures to take to help you start a profitable private label from design to launch are below.

3.2 Understand the costs of private labeling

Before digging deeper into a private label, it's important to consider the initial start-up costs. In comparison to reselling, private tagging is more costly. However, this capital input usually results in a better return on your expenditure in the long term.

Manufacturing

Typical development expenses, such as supplies, processing, manpower, and transportation, would have to be accounted for. You may need to consider the customization charge, too. For customizing a product with your mark, packaging, or specs, most manufacturers will charge a fee.

Brand

Even to design the brand itself, you would require money. To create the logo and package template, you'll definitely want to employ a graphic artist. To stress the voice of your company, you will also want to develop a content strategy.

Marketing

Marketing is a significant part of private labeling. Customers don't know about your company, so to become more noticeable, you need to spread knowledge. A large cost may be generated through ads such as promoted and boosted blogs. A website creator and domain name would presumably both need to be charged for. For any other unforeseen fees or modifications that pop about at the beginning of the start of a new company, you can also add a sizable buffer.

- **Choose the products you want to sell**

The majority of corporations and labels start with a commodity. The brand is how you create your cash and profits. The item is the guiding force of your business. Starting a commodity with your name helps determine your margins, demand, and availability. The brand is the consumer service, but you will need to offer your consumers a valuable product in the end. You would typically choose a branded commodity that you place your own logo on while you market a private label. This suggests that a single generic product begins with your "brand." How do you further build and broaden your branding using that product? You want high-rank and high-margin units when buying a commodity. To lower warehousing and shipping costs, you will want thin, lightweight goods. If the first product you offer doesn't work out or you choose to shift paths, you can still move goods. The aim is to stick less to one commodity than to use product testing as a prism in your overall business and niche instead. You should also accept complimentary commodities with this in mind. If you market key items, you want to think of a range of similar goods that would still blend with your brand when choosing key products. For starters, you can grow inside the travel domain or beverage industry if you sell travel mugs. You will market some eco-friendly home products as well if you sell environmentally efficient cleaning products.

- **Define your target market**

Who is the perfect consumer for you? Who would be more willing to buy your unique product? This can assist you in deciding the sorts of goods you are trying to produce and how you are going to promote such products. The consumer is your market and your brand's secret. Getting a well-defined target demographic is more relevant than ever, considering the current condition of the economy. No one is willing to afford to target everyone. By approaching a niche segment, small enterprises may successfully compete with big firms. Many firms say they are targeting "anyone interested in my services." Others say they are targeting buyers, renters, or stay-at-home moms in small businesses. These priorities are all too common. Targeting a certain market does not mean that you exclude entities that may not follow the standards. Instead, focus marketing helps you to concentrate your advertising money and brand message on a single demographic that is more inclined than other markets to purchase from you. This is a means of meeting prospective consumers and creating a business that is far more accessible, accessible, and effective. For instance, an interior design business might opt to sell to households between the ages of 34 and 63 with incomes of $160,000-plus. The business could opt to approach only those involved in kitchen design remodeling and conventional designs in order to define the segment any better. This business may be broken into two niche markets: parents on the move and baby boomers leaving. It is much simpler to decide where and how to advertise your brand with a well-specified target audience. To help you identify your target market, here are some ideas.

Look at your current customer base.

Who are your new clients, and why are they buying from you? Look for features and desires that are popular. What ones do other businesses carry in? It is also possible that your product/service will also help other individuals like them.

Check out your competition.

What are your adversaries targeting? Who are the clients at present? Don't try the same business. You might discover a niche market they are missing.

Analyze your product/service

Write up a description of each of the product or service specifications. List the advantages it offers next to each function. A graphic artist, for instance, provides high-quality design services. The advantage is the picture of a professional organization. More clients would be drawn to a professional image when they perceive the business as professional and trustworthy. So, basically, attracting more clients and earning more profits is the advantage of high-quality design. When you have your advantages identified, make a list of persons that have a need that suits your benefit. A graphic designer may, for instance, opt to approach organizations involved in increasing their consumer base. Although this is already too common, you now have a foundation on which to proceed.

Choose specific demographics to target.

Find out not only who wants the products or service and also who is most willing to order it. Consider the reasons that follow:

- Location
- Education level

- Occupation
- Gender
- Ethnic background
- Marital or family status
- Age
- Income level
- Ethnic background

Consider the psychographics of your target.

Psychographics is a person's more intimate traits, including:

- Personality
- Values
- Interests/hobbies
- Attitudes
- Lifestyles

- Behavior

Assess how your service or product would blend with the lifestyle of your destination. How and where is the item going to be used by your goal? What characteristics are most enticing to your goal? What media for details does your goal switch to? Can the newspaper read the destination, check online, or attend unique events?

Evaluate your decision

Make sure to consider these issues after you have settled on a target market:

- Are there enough individuals that meet my criteria?
- Is my goal actually going to benefit from my product/service?
- Are they going to have the use for it?
- Do I know what guides my aim to make choices?
- Can they afford my service/product?
- With my post, may I meet them? Are they readily accessible?

Don't smash the goal so far down there. Know, there is more than one niche opportunity you may have. Consider how, for each niche, the marketing message can be different. If you can successfully hit all niches with the same post, then maybe you have broken down the market so much. Also, if you notice that there are only 50 individuals that match all of your requirements, you may need to reevaluate your objective. Finding the right combination is the trick. You might be wondering, "How do I gather all this data?" Attempt to look online for analysis that others have done on your aim. Look for posts and blogs in publications that speak to or around the target group. Check for blogs and sites where thoughts are shared by people in the target market. Check for sample findings, or try doing your own survey. Ask for input from the new clients. The hard part is identifying your target demographic. It is much simpler to find out which platforms you should use to attract them, and what advertisement campaigns can connect with them if you know who you are approaching. You should give it only to people that suit your requirements instead of delivering direct mail to anyone in your ZIP code. In identifying the target demographic, save money and have a greater return on investment.

- **Consider your differentiating factor.**

You've settled on demand and a commodity. Now, what is going to make you distinctive in your business from your competitors? Look at the rivalry. What is their emphasis? And where are they missing? A perfect spot for you to put the brand is the field that they struggle the most. You could find, for example, that all of your rivals have a formal language; with your brand, you might take a goofy and enjoyable tone. In order for it to become a good differentiator, it doesn't have to be a big improvement. The core of your identity becomes your differentiator. Keep in mind that price may also be a defining factor. You would get a different demographic and competition than a cheap or discounted commodity, whether you are quality or luxury product.

- **Create your brand look**

Your "brand" consists of the goods, the demand, and the distinguishers. Yet, it is your material and aesthetic as well. You need a clear emblem that represents the name while private labeling is used. How you are and where the stuff comes from, the logo tells. This emblem can be included in all communications, packaging, and marking. Be sure it's accessible as a corporation and website prior to picking the brand name. This would mean that you do not infringe on any patents or fight with companies with identical names. To build the logo and package template, you'll definitely want to employ a graphic artist. This is the perfect approach to make things look respectable and trustworthy to the private label.

- **Create an experience**

A brand is, ultimately, more than a slogan, though. Your "brand" is how your business is experienced by the client. It's a consistent way for your audience to communicate. You need to work out how consumers can uniquely perceive your brand based on brand differentiation. What is your content going to look like? What could you provide that is unique to the experience of your brand? You may produce visually enticing social media photographs, for instance, that contribute to the lifestyle around your dog collars. Or you should make sure that you react to and respond to any social network statement or post. To keep your label on the edge, you can use special and exclusive packaging. Build an atmosphere, and you can turn your one-time consumers into long-term customers.

- **Find a supplier**

Acting with a good provider is an important aspect of private marking. The manufacturer must have private labeling expertise so they can help you make a return from your products. For a variety of consumers, several overseas factories will produce a standardized commodity and modify such items with private packaging for marking. You collaborate with a retailer, for instance, that produces bottles of water and T-shirts. They have ten buyers, each with their own special emblem written on the bottles, that offer water bottles. A customization and packing fee will normally be paid by the factory.

- **Build the brand**

You have put yourself in a role, built a differentiator, and found a supplier. It's time to start developing your organization now. You have to:

- Name and image copyright.
- Website configuration
- Creating a voice on social media
- Shape an LLC

Just like you would like any other legal corporation, recognize your e-commerce firm. You need yourself, your goods, and your income to be covered. You would also like to start naming the lists with online items. A private label means you don't have to fight for a Buy Package. "With a different page for your branded goods, you hold your own "real estate." In line with the brand background, this is a good chance to customize the listing.

3.3 Choosing the Right Products

Choosing the best market and the right goods to spend your efforts on is the greatest challenge you would have to conquer. This decision is vital to the success or failure of your company. The only biggest mistake you're going to make is selecting a product based on your own interests or personal preferences, particularly if you want to create a genuinely profitable company. You have to provide what other customers want, not what you want. Especially if you are not the type of individual to embrace patterns or the type of individual that is always perceived to be "outside of the box." We can't tell you what products to offer, but we can definitely give you some ideas about how to pick the right ones.

How to choose the right product

Your organization would have an uphill struggle to become profitable without a strong product portfolio. It may seem impossible to try to find out what you are trying to market, with potentially millions of items out there. The item you chose will also pose other concerns that you may need to work on. For starters, shipping may become an issue if you are planning to sell freezers.

Depending on where the clients work, whether you are selling alcohol, there could be regulatory limits. Market analysis can sound daunting, but knowing the product can cater to the people you are going to attract through your site is important. You should monitor the industry dynamics if you already have an understanding of what you intend to do to see how the commodity is actually performing on the market. If you are really not sure what you'd like to offer, trends can still be helpful to you. Business dynamics will offer you an indication about what items consumers are purchasing or are interested in buying at the moment. Look for items that address a dilemma the target group is experiencing. If your consumer is fed up with the current product range, open a unique and better product to deliver them. Choosing a commodity that is not reasonably available nearby or a national brand that is coveted by a region outside of where it is actually accessible may also be a brilliant choice. Another recommendation is to find a service/ product based on your target audience's interests. This may be in the shape of a new TV show that is beginning or a fashion trend. It often applies to aiming for a difference in chances. If you choose a product that many different competitors are already selling, find something that you can do differently or better than everybody else. This can be an enhanced product characteristic, a market that your competitors totally miss, and maybe something in your marketing plan. If you are trying to market a commodity-based on something that is trending at the moment, ensure that you capitalize early on the pattern. There tend to be more individuals who buy the product at the beginning of a trend. Everybody else is now also moving along to the next thing if you get on the hype train at the end of the trend. Do not wait too long to profit on a trend in the market unless you think that you're going to revive a dead trend. When you make your choices, it is important to take into account product turnover. It would take a lot of time and resources on a product range that varies year after year to guarantee that the product selection is held up-to-date and does not include last year's choices, which could no longer be eligible. A reduced churn product would enable you to engage in a more informative website that will be applicable for a longer time span. Don't be frightened of looking at smaller segments and niches of products. Although there may be fewer prospective customers, there will also be less competition, making it easier to get it to the top of the search engines and much more cost-effective in terms of marketing. The right product is an essential part of your success. Take your time and also don't rush into the first good-looking product.

Looking for Product Ideas

There is no need to start a shop without a commodity to sell. Begin with something you already have, or how you can fix your own issues or the challenges of people you meet before you start looking for fresh ideas on what you can sell. There are some ways to consider:

- Which items or niches are you involved in?
- What items are your mates excited about?

- Which challenges do you have with your own life?
- Whose goods can address this?
- What kind of firms are based in your community?
- Can they be translated into a definition online?
- What will organizations in your culture cater to individuals outside of your community?
- In other areas of the planet, what items are trending?
- Is there a need inside your society for them?
- Will you build in your society a market for them?
- Is there a certain sector you like to be interested in if you are confused regarding products? In that industry, what products are popular?
- What items can you find useful from that industry?
- In other online retailers, what items are popular?
- Will this commodity have a niche that you should specialize in in sales?

- What's the social curation website trend?
- Is there an undiscovered thing out there that individuals would want to see open to them?

3.4 Building a Team and Starting your Personal Brand

Choosing the Right Supplier

It can be tricky to pick a supplier for your private label company, but it can help you to realize that there are a variety of suppliers who have been doing this for several years. Some lead the industry in broad industries, and this may be the perfect place to get started in your new company since the goods you offer are already established and have gained appreciation from the market. You can have to trade-off or work in restricted strategies with your profitability, and you need to be careful in reviewing the terms and conditions of each corporation, but each of these can create a backdoor into which you can start a profitable long-term business. Not all private labels are made equally, and to guarantee that your organization is effective, you want to make sure you chose the best provider. There are certain items that your provider wants to provide and some things that are less essential but can have greater convenience. Any of the items you'll be searching for in a provider include:

- Will the retailer have members who are knowledgeable?
- Will the supplier devote them to a particular entity committed to your account?
- Are they invested in being advanced technologically?
- How can you send orders?
- Where are they situated?
- Are they a coordinated business?
- How fast are their orders shipped?

- How are they keeping you throughout the loop on product returns and items out of stock?
- How fast can they send you the tracking details and purchase order?
- What payment types do they approve?
- What kind of fees are they charging?

It may seem impossible to locate the legal firms and distinguish them from the fraudulent as you are searching for a provider. There are some tricks to choosing a decent provider for private labels. One crucial point to bear in mind when you start approaching suppliers is that they could very well be the secret to selecting the best supplier, even though they are not the right match for you. Make sure you always ask every supplier you meet if they can guide you in the appropriate path to reach a supplier that suits your company. As they're in the business, they are sure to have connections that will help you and are typically prepared to share the details. Looking at social media is another way one can improve the chances of having a reliable supplier to deal with. Often, through a family member, neighbor, or acquaintance who might be in the industry or meet someone in the industry, you may find a lead. Any lead is a successful lead, even though it leads to a dead end. In order to strengthen the partnership, you have with your supplier, there are a few items you should do:

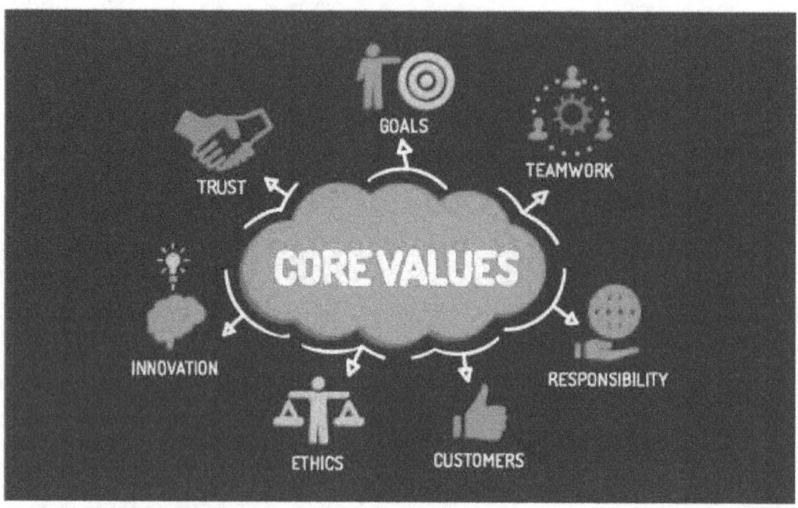

- Pay on time to develop trust and then become a reliable client.
- Set simple and realistic targets if an estimation of the goods you plan to sell in a specified period is requested
- Remember that they have other clients and do not belong to you alone.
- Learn what you need when you put orders to speed up the operation.

- If there is a malfunction, do not accuse the representative, but collaborate with them to find a remedy.

- Knowing somebody on a personal level seems to make them more likely to help you out. Build relationships with your delegate

- Train them to identify what you need, such as fresh product photos and product update updates, items out of stock, and products were withdrawn.

Finding the Right Suppliers and Working with Them

The one crucial part you have to do before you continue the quest for the right suppliers is learned how to say the difference between a true wholesale supplier and a department store that works like one. The manufacturer orders their stock from a genuine wholesaler and delivers far higher deals than a supermarket would. To create a good organization, you need to be able to do all of the following:

Have Access to Exclusive Distribution or Pricing

Being able to negotiate unique product agreements or exclusive prices would offer you the advantage without the need to import or produce your own product to sell online. These are not quick items to arrange, and you can notice that you are still out-priced, and at wholesale rates, some private label brands would still offer the same or equivalent. You need to find a way to persuade the buyers that the commodity you sell is of greater quality than the competitor, whether you can have exclusive distribution, particularly if the competition sells a knock-off product at a cheaper price. This is where the website's "about us" page becomes much more useful as it is a good way to share the fact that you are unique to the product.

Sell at the Lowest Possible Price

You will rob clients from such a chunk of your niche market if you are willing to sell your goods at the lowest costs. The main thing is that since you actually won't be able to appreciate the gain, you are destined to struggle. The low price is not often the primary motivating factor behind the choice of a consumer to shop. Customers seem to choose to invest their cash on the best benefit and lowest cost of a commodity. This suggests that you ought to persuade them that the best decision is to invest a little extra cash in your goods, so there is less downside and more appeal to them.

Add Your Value Outside of the Price

Think in terms of having data that complement the items selected. A real capitalist can fix challenges, and at the same time offering goods at high rates. In your unique niche, make sure you give suggestions and insightful recommendations. Your customer support is one extremely efficient way to bring value to the goods outside of the costs. If you are willing to address all the queries of your consumer without needing to call you and are willing to respond to any emails easily, your store website will stick out from the rest.

Conclusion

A private label is where a person or corporation paying another business to make a commodity without its name, emblem, etc. The person or business then applies to the packaging their name and design. So, what sorts of items should be labeled privately? From skincare and dietary treatments and infant essentials, pet products, and kitchen utensils, pretty much all under the sun. The benefit of private labeling is that nothing innovative needs to be produced or developed by you. You can add your mark on it as long as it's not a proprietary commodity and label it yours. Dropshipping is a convenient method for private-label goods to be distributed. You will find a dropshipping provider if you are an online shop owner who can offer items directly to you and incorporate your branding. Dropshipping is an e-commerce market concept in which no inventory is held by the manufacturer. The retailer, instead, manages the packaging, packing, and delivery of goods to the end customer. In other terms, for dropshipping, the goods are delivered directly to consumers, and they are never used by stores. There is a legitimate explanation for retailers that are involved in flooding their stores with items with their brand name. Third-party suppliers operate at the behest of the supplier, providing full influence over the ingredients and consistency of the goods. In reaction to growing consumer demand for a new feature, smaller stores have the opportunity to move rapidly to bring a private label product into development, whereas larger firms might not be involved in a product or niche category. You should concentrate on creating a reputation before you start your company, one that is recognizable and valued, and a private label benefits both you and the retailer or supplier you select. The first move with your organization is importing the goods you choose to market, products that do not crack easily, which have satisfaction for the customer. The second and most significant move is to make your brand known to current and future clients. The more customers remember your brand, the higher it is possible that your revenue rate will be. Through selecting producers or suppliers who will submit your goods via Private Label, you will help this along. This operates by encouraging the consumer to position their orders with you, then deliver them to the retailer and directly dispatching the product. To sum up, while you are looking to get your brand out and develop a company without leeching on mainstream online marketplace/websites' popularity, a private label makes perfect sense. It will require a bit extra time to select a supplier since you must do the job yourself and guarantee that you work for the right supplier. Still, you will also gain a better profit when you take responsibility for the customer support and are willing to negotiate.

The 9+1 Best Home-Based Business Model of 2021

Find Out how Millennials Have Built Millionaire Businesses from Home with Soap and Candle Making, Natural Cosmetics and much more

By

Amir Lime

Table of Contents

Introduction

Karsanbhai Patel (Patel), the chemist at Mines and Geology Department of the Gujarat Government, produced synthetic powder of detergent phosphate-free in 1969 and began selling this locally. He priced the new yellow powder at 3.50rs per kg. It was at one time when Rs 15 was being charged for Hindustan Lever Limited (HLL) Surf. Soon, in Kishnapur (Gujarat), Patel's hometown, there was a big demand for Nirma. In 10x12 feet space in his home, he began preparing the formula. He had named powder after his daughter's name-Nirupama. On the way to the office by bicycle, about 15 kilometers away, Patel was able to sell around 15-20 packets a day. Thus, the new journey began. Hindustan Lever Limited (HLL) responded in a manner characteristic of many global corporations in the early 1970s, when washing powder Nirma was launched into the market of low-income. "That isn't our business," senior executives said of the new offering. "We don't have to be worried." However very soon, Hindustan Lever Limited (HLL) was persuaded by Nirma's performance in the detergent sector that this wanted to take a closer gaze at the less income market. Low-cost detergents & toilet soaps are almost synonymous with the brand name. Nirma, on the other hand, found that it would've to launch goods targeted at the higher end of the market to maintain the middle-class buyers as they moved up the market. For the luxury market, the firm introduced bathroom soaps. Analysts, on the other hand, claimed Nirma wouldn't be capable of duplicate its performance in the premium market. In the year 2000, the Nirma had a 15 percent share of the toilet soap market and a 30% share of the detergent market. Nirma's revenue for the year ended in March 2000 grew by 17 percent over the previous fiscal year, to 17.17rs. bn, backed by volume development and commissioning of backward integration projects. By 1985, in many areas of the world, washing powder Nirma became one of the most common detergent brands. Nirma was a global consumer company by 1999, with a wide variety of soaps, detergents, & personal care items. Nirma has brought in the latest technologies for the manufacturing facilities in six locations across India, in line with its ideology of delivering premium goods at the best possible costs. The success of Nirma in the intensely competitive market for soaps & detergents was due to its efforts to support the brand, which had been complemented by the sales scope & market penetration. The network of Nirma spread across the country, with over two million outlets of retail and 400 distributors. Nirma was able to reach out to even the smallest villages due to its vast network. Nirma spread to the markets overseas in 1999 after establishing itself in India. Via a joint venture called Commerces Overseas Limited, it made its first foray into Bangladesh. Within a year, the company had risen to the top of Bangladesh's detergent market. Other areas such as Middle East, Russia, China, Africa & additional Asian countries were also intended for the entry of the organization. Nirma became a 17 billion Rs company in 3 decades, beginning as a single-product single-man article of clothing in 1969. Under the umbrella name Nirma, the company had several production plants and a large product range. The mission of the organization to have "Better Product, Better Values and Better Living" added much to its growth. Nirma was able to outshine Hindustan Levers Limited (then HLL) and carve out a niche for oneself in the lower-ends of detergent & market toilet soap. HLL's Surf was the first to be used as a detergent powder in India in 1959. But by the 1970s, merely by making the product available at a reasonable price, Nirma led the demand for detergent powder. Nirma launched its Nirma Beauty soaps to the Indian toilet soap industry in 1990. Nirma had gained a 15% share of 530,000 tons per annum toilet soap industry by 1999, making it India's second-largest producer. Although it was way behind HLL's 65 percent share, the success of Nirma was impressive compared to Godrej, which had an 8 percent share. By 1999-2000, Nirma had already acquired a 38 percent share of India's detergent market of 2.4 million tonnes. For the same period, HLL's market share was 31%. In this book, we will study and analyze the case of Nirma and its rise to the top detergent companies of India. Besides, we will also give profitable ideas and options for starting a lucrative detergent soap, candle making, and natural cosmetics business.

CHAPTER 1: The Nirma Washing Powder's Success Story

The success story of the famous Nirma washing powder began in a small Gujarati farmer's house. We'll tell you about a billionaire father who lost his daughter in a car crash and later discovered a way to get her back to life. When she was alive, only a few people knew of her daughter, but it was the sheer persistence and willpower of this man that made his daughter famous in the world, even though she was no more. This is the story of a man who was born into a poor farming family and turned his daughter's nickname into India's leading detergent, soda ash, and education brand. A man of valor and passion who showed that nothing will hinder you if you have the willpower. Here is the story of **"Sabki Pasand Nirma, Washing Powder Nirma."**

1.1 Invention of Nirma detergent?

Karsanbhai was born in Ruppur, Gujarat, to a farmer's family in 1945. He had earned a bachelor's degree in chemistry by the age of 21. He attempted to do a normal job like his colleagues at first. He served as a lab technician for the Lalbhai Group's New Cotton Mills, which is credited with launching the Indian jeans movement. He also took up a position at the Geology and Mining Department of the Gujarat government after this short stint. The year 1969 marked the start of a turning point in the career trajectory of Karsanbhai. It was at this time that Hindustan Lever Ltd (now Hindustan Unilever) formed a full monopoly on the Indian detergent market under the brand name "Surf." A Surf Pack was sold somewhere from Rs 10-15 back then. The USP was that, unlike normal washing soap bars, it eliminated stains from your clothes and didn't irritate your skin. However, for middle-class families, which had no other choice than to return to the old bar soap, this price point was not affordable. The tycoon in Karsanbhai noticed the issue and devised a plan. A young Karsanbhai will come home from work and dedicate all his time and energy to making a phosphate-free detergent in his yard. He wanted to bear in mind that he needed to produce a detergent with a low manufacturing cost so that everybody could afford it. Karsanbhai utilized a recipe for a yellow-colored detergent powder that could be marketed for a mere Rs 3 after several trials and failures. He chose to name the invention after Nirupama, his daughter. He finally got the formula right one day, and as an after-work business, he began making detergents in his 100-square-foot backyard. He will cycle around the neighborhoods, selling door-to-door homemade detergent packages. Patel set the price of his detergent at Rs. 3, almost a third less than Hindustan Unilever's well-known brand "Surf." The product's high quality and low price made it a success, and it was well-received by many who saw great benefit in purchasing it. Because of the business's high promise, Karsanbhai quit his government job three years later to pursue it full-time. Karsanbhai was so fond of the commodity that he called it Nirma, after his daughter Nirupama's nickname. To make sure that everybody remembers her, he used her picture (the girl in the white frock) on the pack and in TV advertisements. Such was a father's love for his daughter. While Karsanbhai Patel himself was not an MBA graduate, the techniques he adopted to expand his company left marketers bewildered and amazed. 'Nirma' was not only a game-changer but also a trendsetter for several small companies. Here are a couple of 'Washing Powder Nirma's' management lessons.

1.2 Karsanbhai Patel's sale policy for Nirma detergent

Karsanbhai Patel agreed to start marketing it once the product had a strong formula. On his cycle, he used to go door-to-door and neighborhood-to-neighborhood every day for three years, pitching the detergent. As it was a brand new product, if they found the product poor, he gave his consumers a money-back guarantee. Nirma has been the cheapest detergent in Ahmedabad at the time. As a result, Karsanbhai's product was an immediate hit. He left his government job three years later and set up a store in Ahmedabad to carry out this full-time enterprise. In some areas of Gujarat, his brand was doing very well, but there was a need to expand its scope. At the time, the standard was to offer the product to retailers on credit. This was a huge gamble because if the product didn't sell, Karsanbhai would have had to close down the company. At that time, he chose to try something different. He planned to spend a little money on advertising. These commercials, with their catchy jingles, were directed at housewives. And this bet paid off well. Nirma became a famous household brand and it had to be purchased by people. He did, however, remove 90% of the stock from the market at this time. Potential buyers had asked for the detergent at their local retailers for about a full month but would have to return empty-handed. During this time, retail store owners flocked to Karsanbhai, demanding that the detergent supply be increased. After another month, he eventually decided. Nirma was able to take over the sales and even beat Surf at their own game due to this approach. It went on to become the country's highest-selling detergent. It remained India's largest-selling detergent even after a decade,

1.3 Invest In Research and Development

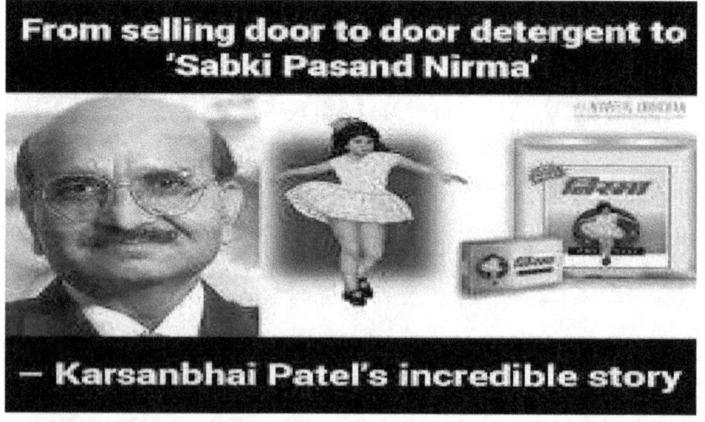

Karsanbhai Patel had little means and was not a man born with a silver spoon in his mouth. Karsanbhai loved experimenting with chemicals after completing a B.Sc. in Chemistry at the age of 21 and then working as a laboratory technician. He noticed that only MNCs in India were selling detergents and there was no economy brand detergent for the country. His excitement about bridging the distance grew, sensing a massive opening, and Karsanbhai began experimenting with chemicals. He quickly succeeded in manufacturing a detergent of high quality at a much cheaper price, which was an immediate success in the industry. Every good product needs a substantial expenditure in time, resources, and commitment in research and development.

1.4 No Higher Costs

Nirma had rewritten the rules of the game within a short time, by delivering high-quality goods at an unprecedentedly low price. Nirma's success was due to its cost-cutting policy. Patel had concentrated from the very beginning on delivering high-value goods at the lowest price possible. The corporation sought to keep improving efficiency while reducing prices. Nirma sought out captive processing plants for raw materials to keep production costs to a minimum. This led to the backward integration initiative, as part of which, at Baroda and Bhavnagar, which became operational in 2000, two state-of-the-art plants were established. This also led to a reduction in raw-material prices. Ahead of time and at a much smaller cost than anticipated, the two new plants were completed. The Baroda plant's second phase was finished 6 months ahead of schedule and at a cost of Rs.2.5 billion compared to the initial projected cost of Rs. 2.8 billion. Compared to the initial projected cost of Rs. 10.36 billion, the Bhavnagar plant was finished in a record period of 2 years at a cost of Rs.9.86 billion.

This plant had a workforce of just 500 employees. Concerning Nirma's plant, Tata Chemical's plant, which had around twice the amount, employed ten times the number of workers. Almost 65000 tpa of N-Paraffin was produced by the Baroda plant for Linear Alkyl Benzene (LAB) and Synthetic detergents. Similarly, almost 4.20,000 tpa of soda ash could be produced by the Bhavnagar facility. Akzo Nobel Engineering in Holland produced the Akzo Dry Lime technology used in this factory. The plant had 108 kilometers of salt bunds, which would assist in the potential development of vacuum iodized salt. Patel said, "We have a processing potential of three lakh tons of pure salt. No one in the world had a related plant, but Tata Salt." Nirma had reduced its distribution costs by obviating the need for middlemen. The item went to the dealer straight from the manufacturer. Hiren K Patel (Hiren), CMD, explained to Nirma Customer Care Ltd., "An order is placed and the truck immediately leaves. It's similar to a bank account. We're sending stock, they're sending money." In states like Tamil Nadu, Andhra Pradesh, and southern Karnataka, the company-maintained depots, as it was often difficult to bring stocks to these regions. Stocks were shipped directly from the plants in states like Madhya Pradesh and Uttar Pradesh. In March 2000, Nirma opted for in-house packaging and printing by obtaining Kisan Factories at Moriya, near Ahmedabad, in a further cost-cutting exercise. Nirma hoped that this would increase the packaging's quality.

1.5 Be Proactive in your approach as it is beneficial for the business

Karsanbhai Patel was the only person who started this business and starting selling Nirma. He was educated and had a government career, but he was never afraid of selling door-to-door detergent. He was diligent in doing something and knew that the company was tiny and bootstrapping, so he had to consider everything and anything about his business that could be fruitful. There is no such thing as a small or large undertaking. And if you are the CEO, you should embrace the obligations that are valuable to the company without guilt.

1.6 Provide Customers with 'Value for Money'

Customers noticed the advantages of purchasing Nirma, and it became an immediate success. They considered the standard to be at par with the giant Surf brand, but to take advantage of the same perks, they just had to pay one-third of the amount. Customers would only appreciate the product if you show them the advantages and give them decent value for their money.

1.7 Define Your Segment

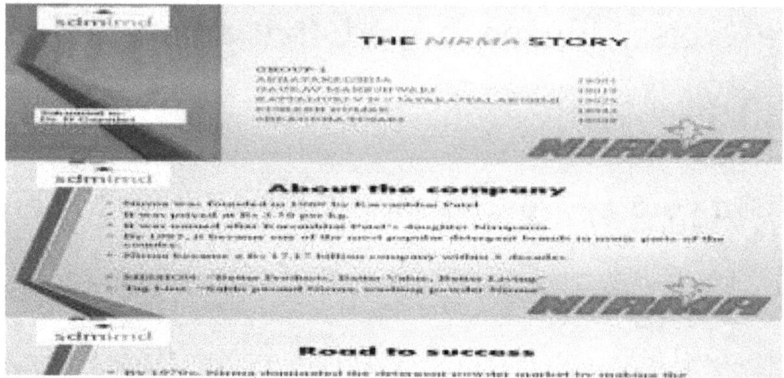

Karsanbhai Patel identified the target segment for his detergent almost as soon as he found the magical formula. He realized that a luxury brand sold in tier 1 cities was the alternative Surf brand, so he concentrated on marketing his brand in tier 2-3 cities. He priced his detergent low and made it a mass brand to get more consumer traction. People from the lower middle class and middle class quickly adopted the product, and it quickly rose in popularity. Where most firms adopted the conventional top-down strategy, i.e., spreading from metro towns to rural cities, Nirma did the reverse and changed the whole game. It is really important to evaluate the competitors for every company and define the most lucrative segment.

1.8 Focus on Building a Brand

It was failing to find vendors outside the city in the early 80s, although the commodity was approved on a small scale in Ahmedabad. Since clients were unaware of its presence, retailers were wary of keeping the detergent in their stores. It resulted in overdue payments, return on inventory, and large business losses. Karsanbhai Patel came up with a good publicity approach to handle the situation and launched a TV advertisement campaign. The popular "Washing powder Nirma, detergent tikiya Nirma" jingle became an anthem for the company and customers began to equate Nirma as a strong brand. The demand for Nirma soon peaked, and with his products, Patel flooded the retail stores. A good brand decreases a buyer's potential risk and increases the company's bargaining power.

1.9 Astutely Manage the Brand Wars

Nirma also had innovative marketing campaigns. Nirma successfully spread the name to other product segments in the mid-nineties, such as premium detergents (Nirma Mega Detergent Cake and Washing Powder), premium toilet soaps, and (Nirma Sandal, Nima Premium, Nirma Lime Fresh). In both the economy and luxury markets, it maintained its initial pricing and marketing plans. In 2000, with Nirma Beauty Shampoo, Nirma Shikakai, and Toothpaste, the firm entered the hair care market. Soaps, unlike detergents, were a private-care commodity. Many consumers had strong emotional attachments with their soap products. Furthermore, HLL segmented the market by price, fragrance appeal, and brand personality. So, against Lifebuoy, Nirma put Nirma Wash, Nirma Beauty Soap against Lux, Nima Rose against

Breeze7, and Nima Lime against Jai Lime. Explaining how Nirma hoped to win this match, playing by the rules of HLL, Hiren said"Worldwide, there are only four or five channels that account for most of the soaps sold: floral, fashion, fitness, freshness." With the relevant scents, Nirma manufactured high-fatty-matter soaps and priced them much lower than other brands. As a result, the 'sub-premium' section was born. The game of controlling the geographical variety of market desires was also perfected by Nirma. The North, for instance, favored pink soaps, and green ones were favored by the South. In the South, sandal soaps were more common. Initially, the company's promotional budget, relative to other FMCG firms, was very poor. In contrast to the usual 6-10 percent, Nirma spent just 1.25-2 percent of its sales on ads. The firm used starlets such as Sangeeta Bijlani, Sonali Bendre, and Riya Sen, who were comparatively unknown at the time, to endorse soaps. The promotional messages were both transparent and centered on the product's benefits. Nirma still chose to first put the item on the shelf, get reviews, and then create a lasting ad campaign. Nirma used its tried-and-true tool, price, to introduce toilet soaps and detergents in the premium market. In these divisions, the company intended to rely on quantities as well. However, the margins granted to retailers had shifted. Unlike economic goods, where the cost advantages were passed on to customers, this advantage was passed on to retailers by Nirma. It provided them with massive profit margins. For instance, it offered 52 percent for Nirma premium soap and an incredible margin of 140 percent for Nirma shampoo. In the luxury segment of the soap industry, observers were pessimistic about Nirma's chances of success.

Unlike detergents, the demand for soaps and shampoos was incredibly fragmented. There were only 15-20 brands, and it was hard to get a considerable market share for any soap. This market was also less price sensitive. So, it was hard for any enterprise to support itself on price alone. Analysts thought that shifting the brand value of Nirma would take years. According to a survey conducted by Nirma's marketing agency, Samsika Marketing Consultancy, Nirma was viewed as a low-cost brand. Many people were almost afraid to say they used it. Nirma published corporate advertisements worth Rs 10 bn in India in the late nineties to shed this image. Analysts claim that the fast-growing shampoo market is a safer investment than luxury soaps. Just 30% of the population in India used shampoo, with more than 70% of this group living in urban areas. However, according to some researchers, while the rural market's presumed potential was very high, it was difficult to convince rural folk to use shampoos in actual practice. A further concern faced by Nirma was that of insufficient facilities. While it had a good presence in the smaller towns and villages, it lacked the requisite network for urban centers to penetrate. As a result, Nirma's foray into high-end soaps and shampoos proved to be a flop.

1.10 Diversify the Portfolio

For low-income groups, Nirma began with a low-cost detergent, but later introduced products for higher-income groups, such as Nirma Sandal soap, Nirma Beauty soap, etc.

Not just that, but in 2003, Karsanbhai Patel formed Nirma University to diversify the company's brand portfolio. The brand is currently exploring its options in the cement industry to grow its market. Diversifying the portfolio decreases the company's potential risk of loss while still allowing it to serve a broader variety of consumers.

1.11 Conclusion

While Nirma was best known as a manufacturer of goods for the low-cost economy, it was popular in the middle and upmarket segments. Yet rivalry was also growing at the same time. Although HLL continued to be a major threat, offensive initiatives were also introduced by P&G and Henkel SPIC. In the detergent and washing powder market, participants from the unorganized field were also introduced to the rivalry. Patel was confident of tackling the rivalry, though. "He added, "We keep the price line and the happy customer returns to us normally. Based on its growth strategy, the company has risen in demand and volume in the last three decades: "A buyer is not looking for one-time frills or feel-good variables. The landlord, on the other hand, is searching for a long-term solution to his or her issues." Karsanbhai Patel, who began with a vision of making his daughter famous through his brand and ended up being one of the greatest entrepreneurs of all time, exemplifies the relevance of this quotation. He began with an aim of creating his daughter famous through his brand and ended up becoming one of the greatest entrepreneurs of all time. His name not only gained tremendous respect but also became a trendsetter for many new firms. The brand has taught young entrepreneurs many useful lessons and has proven to be a valuable resource for the region. Karsanbhai Patel has shown that no goal is too lofty if you have the ambition and zeal to achieve it.

1.12 What Karsanbhai Patel and Nirma detergent did for the Indian Economy

Nirma's meteoric growth in prominence culminated in the introduction of a new economic market for detergent powder. It was of good quality and was inexpensive. Plus, contrary to the others, the fact that it was manufactured without phosphates made it the most environmentally-friendly detergent. In comparison, a labor-consuming process was the process of producing the detergent. And thus, Nirma went on to hire more than 14,000 workers and became the country's leading employer.

1.13 Karsanbhai Patel's ventures other than the Nirma detergent

Karsanbhai wanted to grow his FMCG business after Nirma dominated the detergent industry. Nirma launched its line of toilet soaps, beauty soaps, and even shampoos in the premium market. While the latter venture failed, one of their products, edible salt Shudh, is still available and doing well. Overall, Nirma has a 20 percent market share in soap cakes and a 35 percent market share in detergents. That isn't it, however. In 1995, Karsanbhai Patel founded the Nirma Institute of Technology in Ahmedabad. Later, it became one of Gujarat's most prestigious engineering schools. After that, the whole structure was merged under the Nirma University of Science and Technology, which is supervised by the Nirma Education and Research Foundation, and in 2003, the entire structure was unified under the Nirma University of Science and Technology. This is overseen by the Nirma Education and Research Foundation. Since 2004, Karsanbhai's CSR initiative, Nirmalabs education, has aimed to train and incubate entrepreneurs. Karsanbhai Patel has now turned over the reins of his profitable company to his two sons. Pratibha Patil, the then-President of India, bestowed the Padma Shri on him in 2010. Nirma is now the world's biggest manufacturer of soda ash, and the company has been privately owned since 2012. Karsanbhai Patel invested his huge fortune on a six-seat chopper in 2013, which cost Rs 40 crore. After Gautam Adani (Adani Group) and Pankaj Patel (Zydus Group), he became the third Ahmedabad-based industrialist to purchase a helicopter. Nirma, on the other hand, is still one of India's most popular detergents. And the jingles will live on forever.

CHAPTER 2: Start a Profitable Soap Making Business

As a soap manufacturer, you'll create your recipes for soaps and probably other personal cleaning and beauty products. Ecommerce, farmers markets, arts events, wholesale positioning in spas and boutiques, and even door-to-door sales are all options for selling the goods. You'll test several solutions and see if you can find a steady stream of clients. Learn how to launch a soap-making company of your own.

Steps for starting a soap making business

You've uncovered the ideal market opportunity and are now prepared to take the next step. There's more to launching a company than simply filing papers with the government. We've put together a list of steps to help you get started with your soap-making business. These measures will ensure that the new company is well-planned, legally compliant, and properly registered.

Plan your business

As an entrepreneur, you must have a well-thought-out strategy. It will assist you in figuring out the additional data of your organization and uncovering any unknowns. Given below are some key points to consider:

What are the startup and recurring costs?

Who is the targeted audience?

What is the maximum price you will charge from the customers?

What would you name your company?

What are the costs involved in opening a soap-making business?

You've got a good start if you have a kitchen or workspace as well as a few simple kitchen utensils. Making soap isn't an expensive business to undertake, but you would need to invest in some basic equipment. Ingredients cost at least $200. Lye and fats or oils are used to make soap. That's a good start, but it'll be your special formula that sets you apart. For superior feel, fragrance, and lather, you can use coconut oil, olive oil, almond oil, and several fragrance oils, extracts, and natural additives. To keep materials costs down and simplify production, you could start with only one or two simple recipes. Equipment for producing soap will cost around $300. Your equipment specifications will be determined by the type of soap-making you do. Hot process, cold process, rebatching, and melt and pour are the four basic forms of processing, and each needs different equipment. But, regardless of the route you take, you'll almost definitely need soap molds, packing, and shipping items. You can get your basic ingredients, additives, equipment, and supplies from several online retailers. Marketing software will cost up to $750. A professional-looking website with enticing product images is key to the company's growth. Since your online consumers can't touch or smell your goods, they must be able to judge the good quality of what they see. That means recruiting a graphic designer and web developer to help you make the best out of your logo and online presence is a smart investment. To express your love and dedication to product quality, your visual imagery will be carried through in your labeling and branding. Skilled services will cost up to $200. Is it legal in your state and society for you to run this sort of business from home? Before you put up your shingle, meet with a lawyer for a quick consultation. The Handcrafted Soap & Cosmetics Guild charges a membership fee of $100 per year (HSCG). Small-batch soap makers will benefit from this organization's preparation, funding, and useful networking opportunities. Insurance for general liability and product liability would cost $265-$375 a year. This is also accessible via the HSCG.

What are the ongoing expenses for a soap-making business?

The consumable commodity materials you'll need for ongoing development would be your greatest ongoing expense. Your increasing variable expenses would be more than offset by a rise in revenue if you've priced your offering correctly.

Who is the target market?

While women make up the majority of the demand for homemade soaps, some firms have had success selling male-oriented soap scents. You may approach consumers who admire your product's consistency and luxury, or those who only purchase organic or vegan goods. Customers will note the difference in quality among your soaps and those sold on the shelves of a traditional supermarket.

How does a soap-making business make money?

In the majority of the cases, all of your revenue shall be derived from the products you make or sell.

How much can you charge customers?

Your goods could be sold for $5 or $6 a bar. This is more than your consumers are likely to spend for mass-produced retail soaps, but your product has a high perceived value. Other price points can be met by providing discounts on multiple orders, marketing multi-bar bundles, and extending the product range. Look at local rivals' websites to see what they're costing and how that would impact the pricing. Will you charge more to suggest a higher-end product range, or will you charge less to compensate for the lower per-unit sales margin with higher volume?

How much profit can a soap-making business make?

There are a few well-known soap makers who began their careers in the same way you did. Take, for example, Burt's Bees. Others in your business run it as a side venture, something between a crafts hobby and a modestly profitable business. You will go as far as your dedication, imagination, promotional skills, and hard work can take you, as with many home-based companies.

How can you make your business more profitable?

Many soap makers diversify their product range to include more exotic soaps (goat's milk soap is one example) or complementary goods. Making candles is a natural progression for soap makers who still use a hot process. Others are involved in home fragrances, lip balms, hair care, and even pet products. Focus on what else will cater to the consumer base when speaking about expanding your product mix. Many companies aim to maximize their net income by lowering the cost of goods produced. Growing the earnings by issuing bigger batches at a time is a cost-effective technique.

2.1 What will you name your business?

Choosing the correct name is vital and daunting. If you own a sole proprietorship, you should start using a separate company name from your own. We suggest reviewing the following references before filing a company name:

The state's business records

Federal and state trademark records

Social media sites

Web domain availability

It's important to have your domain name registered before anyone else does.

2.2 Form a legal entity

The sole proprietorship, partnership, limited liability company (LLC), and corporation are the most traditional corporate structures. If your soap manufacturing company is used, creating a legitimate business entity such as an LLC or corporation prevents you from being found legally accountable.

Register for taxes

Before you can start doing business, you'll need to apply for several state and federal taxes. You would need to apply for an EIN to pay for taxation. It's very basic and free.

2.3 Small Business Taxes

Depending on which business arrangement you select, you can have various taxation choices for your corporation. There could be state-specific taxes that apply to your business. In the state sales tax guides, you can read more about state sales taxes and franchise taxes.

2.4 Open a business bank account & credit card

Personal wealth security necessitates the use of dedicated company banking and credit accounts. If your personal and corporate accounts are combined, your personal properties (such as your house, vehicle, and other valuables) are put at risk if your company-issued. This is referred to as piercing the corporate veil in business law. Furthermore, learning how to create company credit will help you receive credit cards and other borrowings under your business's name (rather than your own), lower interest rates, and more credit lines, among other advantages.

2.5 Open a business bank account

This protects your assets from those of your business, which is essential for personal wealth security, as well as making accounting and tax reporting simpler.

2.6 Get a business credit card

It will help you achieve the following benefits:

It builds the company's credit background and will be beneficial for raising capital and profit later on.

It lets you differentiate personal and business expenditures by placing all of your business's costs under one account.

Set up business accounting

Understanding your business's financial results includes keeping track of your different costs and sources of revenue. Maintaining correct and comprehensive reports also makes annual tax filing even simpler.

2.7 Obtain necessary permits and licenses

Failure to obtain required permits and licenses will result in hefty fines or even the closure of your company. If you intend to market homemade soaps, you must first acquire a business license.

2.8 State & Local Business Licensing Requirements

Operating a handmade soap company can necessitate the procurement of some state permits and licenses. Furthermore, several states have varying laws governing the manufacturing of cosmetics and other body care goods. Visit the SBA's guide to state licenses and permits to read more about your state's licensing criteria.

2.9 Labor safety requirements

It is essential to comply with all Occupational Safety and Health Administration protocols. Pertinent requirements include:

Employee injury report

Safety signage

2.10 Certificate of Occupancy

A Certificate of Occupancy is normally required for businesses that operate out of a specific location (CO). All requirements concerning building codes, zoning rules, and local requirements have been followed, according to a CO. If you're thinking about renting a space, keep the following in mind:

Securing a CO is normally the landlord's duty.

Before signing a contract, make sure your landlord has or can get a legitimate CO for a soap-making operation.

A new CO is often needed after a significant renovation. If your company will be renovated before opening, add wording in your lease agreement that specifies that lease payments will not begin before a valid CO is issued.

If you intend to buy or build a place:

You would be responsible for securing a legal CO from a local government body.

Review all building codes and zoning standards for your soap-making business's place to ensure that you'll comply and eligible to get a CO.

2.11 Trademark & Copyright Protection

It is wise to protect your interests by applying for the required trademarks and copyrights if you are creating a new product, idea, brand, or design. The essence of legal standards in distance education is continually evolving, especially when it comes to copyright laws. This is a regularly revised database that can assist you with keeping on top of legal specifications.

2.12 Get business insurance

Insurance, including licenses and permits, are necessary for your company to run safely and legally. In the case of a covered loss, corporate insurance covers your company's financial well-being. There are several insurance schemes tailored for diverse types of companies with various risks. If you're not sure what kinds of risks your company might face, start with General Liability Insurance. This is the most popular form of coverage required by small companies, so it's a good place to start.

2.13 Learn more about General Liability Insurance

Workers' Compensation Insurance is another essential insurance scheme that many companies need. When your company hires staff, your state may mandate you to carry the Workers' Benefits Package.

2.14 Define your brand

Your company's brand is what it stands for, as well as how the general public perceives it. A good name would set the company apart from the market.

How to promote & market a soap making business

Look for areas where you can stand out. Try having a larger-than-usual bar of soap or one that is formulated to last longer. Perhaps you should market a six-pack of sampler soaps in smaller sizes so that your customers can check out your whole product range and pick their preferences. Consider an uncommon fragrance or texture additive for applying to your soaps to make them stand out. When you've found a winning design, publicize it on your website and social media. Also, if you're showing your soaps at an exhibition, bring some unwrapped samples of your entire product line so consumers can touch them, see what they're made of, feel their textures, and experience the various scents.

How to keep customers coming back

bear in mind that you're offering an aesthetic experience. Make sure your logo, labels and packages, and the name of your product line all cater to consumers looking for a low-cost luxury experience. One benefit is that the more your consumers like your stuff, the faster they can consume it and require more. Ensure that you retain contact with your clients and that they are aware of how to contact you. Request email addresses from all of your clients to obtain their approval to send out a monthly e-newsletter or catalog. It's important not to bother someone with so many promotional newsletters, but a monthly newsletter will keep consumers updated on all of the new items you have to sell. You might want to add a toll-free phone number for orders as your company expands.

Establish your web presence

Customers can learn more about your business and the goods or services you deliver by visiting your website. One of the most successful ways to build your web presence is through press releases and social media.

2.15 Soap Making Plan

If you live in the jungle and love your body odor, you would not need soap. It is a regular need and one of the common goods. As a result, soap has a huge demand. There are various varieties of soaps available due to the wide range of skin types. Soaps are manufactured in a multitude of ways to suit the needs of all. One of the most promising FMCGs is soap production. Perhaps this is why so many people are drawn to this sector year after year. Every day, in a country like India, there is a massive demand for soap. However, there are only a few competitors in the business. We have a few ideas for you if you want to launch your own soap company. Let's get this started.

Tips for soap making using the cold process method

Soap making is easy at the most fundamental level. The cold process approach is the most common way to produce soap. It's "cold" because the ingredients aren't heated before being combined. Using the "hot process" technique, you can make soap with heat. We will use the cold process. Soap is made by mixing fats and oils with a lye and water solution in the most basic form. Soap is made from a combination of water, lye, fats, and oils. The fun starts as you change the components and quantities of the various materials. But, to keep things simple, note that soap is essentially a solution of fats and oils, lye, and water. It's as plain as that.

Is making soap without lye possible?

Is it possible to produce soap without lye? Not at all. Soap bases that can be heated and poured into molds can be purchased. You didn't have to use lye to make the base as everyone else did. However, you have no idea what's in those bases. Sodium hydroxide is the lye used to produce bar soap. Soft soaps are made of potassium hydroxide. Leaching lye from wood ashes is an easy way to create it. This form of lye results in a smoother soap. Unless you have access to a chemical supply house, lye is typically difficult to come by locally. It is, however, simple to put an order. Lye is highly caustic, and it can sear the skin and strip color from whatever surface it comes into contact with. If it gets into your eyes, it will blind you. This is a toxic drug and can never be used in a place where children may reach it. Adults, on the other hand, would have no trouble with the lye if they take simple precautions. When dealing with lye, please wear safety goggles. Long sleeves and protective gloves are also recommended. Leave lye or lye mixtures unattended at all times. Uncured soap should be used similarly to lye.

Fats and oils required for making the cold process soap

Another fundamental to producing soap can be found here. To turn oils and fats into soap, different quantities of lye are needed. Every fat that is likely to be used in soap making has a known amount of time it takes to turn oil or fat into soap. Simply look up the amount of lye needed to produce soap from a certain oil in a table. The volume of lye used in each recipe is then determined based on the oils used. Using a little less lye than is needed to transform all of the oils into soap. This is achieved as a precautionary step to ensure that all of the lye is absorbed during the process. The lye discount is the volume of lye used that is reduced. It's normal to use around 5% less lye than is needed to completely transform the oils into soap. Coconut, palm, and olive oils are the most common oils used in soap making. If you just use those three oils to make soap, you will make amazing results. Each of these oils has its collection of characteristics that make it useful as a soaping oil. You can produce a soap with only one of the oils, but the results won't be as strong as if you used all three. This is why. If you want a lot of bubbles in your soap, coconut oil is the way to go. It's the root of a slew of big, light bubbles. However, soap made entirely of coconut oil cleans so well that it extracts much of the oil from the skin, leaving it dry. This is why it can only account for about 30% of the soap oils. Palm oil is important for hard, long-lasting bars, but it isn't as clean or bubbly as coconut oil. This fat is often referred to as "vegetable tallow," but it is similar to beef tallow in any way. If you don't want to eat meat fats, use them instead of beef fat. Then you should ask about olive oil. Just olive oil is used to produce castile soap conventionally. If you've ever used this form of soap, you know how good it is as a skin conditioner. It's amazing. However, if olive oil is the only oil used in the soap, the effect is tiny little bubbles and bars that fade away quicker than you'd like. As a result, this type of oil is only used to make up about 40% of the oils in a recipe. Granted, soap can be made from almost any form of fat or oil, and there are several alternatives.

Adding ingredients for premium luxury results

If you choose to use other oils, just apply a small amount during the final stages of the soap-making process. you'll find that you can use almond oil in your example recipe. Simply raise the amount of olive oil in the formula and leave out the almond oil. It was chosen because it brings a little more to the bar's feel and quality. Soap can be used for a lot more than just producing pure soap. All of the additives are what make soap production so exciting. Clays, natural oils, medicinal products, colors, patterns, and a slew of other alternatives are available as additives. The first step to perfect soap is to get the fundamentals correctly, which can be achieved fast and effectively. After learning the fundamentals of soap manufacturing, the soap manufacturer progresses to using a range of exotic ingredients.

How to make soap?

We'll go into the fundamentals of how the soap is made. Bear in mind that this is just the first step. Following that, you may need additional materials and a special recipe to distinguish the product from competitors.

Ingredients

Given below are the following ingredients that would be required for preparing soap:

Take 2/3 cup of coconut oil (that will create lather) and the same amount of olive oil. Moreover, 2/3 cup almond, safflower oil, or grape seed will also be needed.

Then you'll need a quarter cup of lye, which is sodium hydroxide in its purest form. Finally, you'll require 3/4 cup of cool water that is distilled or pure.

You'll also need oatmeal, aloe vera gel, cornmeal, clay, salt, and any other items you choose to use.

Instructions

Listed below are the step-by-step directions that you must follow in the preparation of soap:

Put on your gloves and pour lye and water into a canning jar. Allow them to sit for a few minutes after they've been stirred gently and the water has begun to clear.

Now pour in the oil from the pint jar. Then Stir well, then put the jar in a warm pan of the water that is bubbling (and/or you may microwave it, when you do, place temperature to one hundred and twenty degrees F).

Remove the lye after that is finished. Allow the lye to cool. Remove pint jar & allow your oil to cool as well. Both can achieve a temperature of 95 to 105 degrees Fahrenheit. If the temperature drops below 95 degrees F, the soap will begin to crumble.

Pour them into a mixing bowl until they've hit the ideal temperature and whisk until fully combined. After stirring for five minutes, mix it with an immersion blender.

Then, to make the soap special, apply herbs, essential oils, & any other things that go with it. They can be thoroughly combined so they appear coarse. Place them in molds & cover with a towel.

After a day check the soap and let it stay for an additional 12 to 24 hours if it's either warm or soft.

When the soaps are fully cured, wrap them in the paper wax & lock them in an airtight jar for a week. Since this soap contains oil on its own, we'll need an airtight jar. As a consequence, interaction with air will cause it to pick up debris and dust.

Soap making machine and price

fiber covered mixing machine will cost you at least about US$ 1000. This price includes a fiber-covered mixing machine capable of producing 200 kilograms of detergent powder.

Where to get soap making machine?

Online, you can buy a soap-manufacturing machine. Soap manufacturing machines are available from several online retailers. These websites sell the requisite appliances, including the microwave, blender, wrapper, mold, and labeler, also the main device. A soap-making unit, for example, can be bought for the US $ 5000. This item can be used to produce toilet soaps and detergent cakes. If you're searching for something less costly, say under the US $ 1500 apiece, you can easily find it on the market. It can be used to produce soap for bathing purposes. There are also other products of varying price points. However, the budget may start at one dollar an item. You'll get a good detergent maker for this amount.

Soap making raw material and price

The Soap-making ingredients may be bought for a very cheap price. It is much less costly if you buy them in bulk. If you may get the price correct upfront, the rest of the company will be a breeze later on. As a consequence, we prefer bulk raw materials. Alkali and fat are the two main raw materials used to produce soap. the raw material which is most commonly used in soap manufacture is sodium hydroxide. Potassium hydroxide, on the other hand, maybe used. The latter makes a soap that is more soluble in water. As a result, potassium hydroxide creates "warm soap." Locally, raw products are available at a reduced quality. You can discover raw materials for manufacturing soaps online or in your neighborhood with a fast Google search. People typically buy this locally so it cuts the price even further. Rest assured that rates can differ depending on your needs. It depends solely on how much you're making & how much of the raw material you'll need. Caustic soda costs about US $ 150-250 per metric ton on the market. The price of 1000 grams of laundry soap ranges between US$1 and $1.25.

Soap making formulae

legitimate chemical formulae for the soap's $C_{17}H_{35}COONa$. Its chemical name is thus sodium stearate. However, it is important to note that it's for the common soap that is used for personal purposes only. For the detergents, there are normally long chains of carboxylic acid as well as sulfonate salts or ammonium salt.

2.16 Soap selling process

Let us now go through the packaging, distribution, marketing, and promotion processes.

Colorful wrappings

Choose a bright & eye-catching label that will guarantee that the product is noticed. To set it apart from the competition, style it & use the proper design.

Branding

Make the most of this opportunity to build your brand through packaging. Choose a design that you think best reflects your business.

Go simple

Today's entrepreneurs aim for simplicity. Examine the performance of POP displays as well. If they don't live up to your standards, it's time to make a change.

Soap marketing strategy

You can use the following strategies for marketing soap:

Email marketing

And the ones who also sign up for your offer are truly interested in the soaps, email marketing is the perfect way to market. It’s also becoming highly customizable and cost-efficient these days.

Blogging

The next logical move is to start blogging. You'll need to hunt down some prominent bloggers who may help you spread the word about the business. You may even invite them to write a review on their blog about a sample of the product.

Social media

Due to availability of the social media, it is now easier to create a brand. Furthermore, guess what? It’s the shortest and least expensive alternative. The secret is to make something go viral. this could be the merchandise, online presence, or your ads.

2.17 Soap making supplies

To make it function properly, you'll need some modernized tools equipment, as well as a lot of the space. You will need to find rental space to make the soap. Some of the typical things you'll need to get started include cyclone, mixing vessels, perfumers, blowers, reactors, furnaces, weighing scales, and blenders.

2.18 Marketing area for soap

The marketing region you select will be decided by the audience you're targeting. You would be able to segment your customers depending on age and demographic in social media marketing. Your marketing field can be decided by the type of soap you sell. If you're selling detergent cakes, for example, they're mainly aimed at homemakers of different ages. As a consequence, you will show the commercial depending on age & gender. Marketing is successful on a variety of measures. It simply depends upon whether you've online or a physical company. In any case, it's better to entrust this to a practitioner.

2.19 Total investment

The Investment isn't based on raw materials. Just As mentioned above, different raw materials are used for personal and detergent soaps. Therefore investment will be different for each category.

You must take into consideration the size and place of the business for starting the business. So You need minimum money of US $ 20,000to purchase the machinery along with primary raw materials -if you decide to start with little.

Raw materials shall cost the US $ 2500 per month. Moreover, making unit rentals would charge not less than the US $ 1000 per month. In addition to the above-mentioned costs, the salary of the plant manager is expected to be around the US $ 500. Equipment shall cost around the US $ 10,000 or more.

In addition to the above prices, you need the US $ 500 for license & registration. Moreover, you will need another US $ 800 to cover the accidental coverage. the Marketing might cost you approximately US $ 500 per month.

2.20 Selling price

Supply, materials, brand, packaging, and other factors impact soap pricing. When you're only starting, keep the rates comparable to those of your rivals.

Prices are determined by several factors. A lower-cost soap is generally assumed to be of lower quality. As a result, we won't keep prices very low about market prices.

Additionally, too high prices could decrease overall demand. As a consequence, we will arrive at the golden middle & retain it just marginally, so at all, below current levels.

2.21 Profit margin

Measure profit margins through factoring in your annual manufacturing expenses. You must also remember manpower, raw materials, utilities, and maintenance costs.

This business has a high-profit margin, but it also has a lot of competition from well-known brands. As a result, profit margins would be dictated by the price of the goods.

Know more about your rivals' prices and, as a result, determine which would give the greatest return - find the "golden value point" for the sales.

2.22 Precaution

It is important to obtain insurance. it is why, in addition to other necessities, insurance must still be part of the investment.

Another crucial step's to understand the company's legal framework. Obtain both the "consent to establish" and "consent to operate."

2.23 Risk

In the soap industry, the risk is not creating a large enough brand to compete with the rivals. There are a lot of competitors in the business, so making a name for your company can be challenging.

Another danger is that the company will collapse due to a lack of consumer awareness. To run a good soap company, you must first select the right market.

2.24 Conclusion

Soap production, as satisfying as this is, necessitates thorough study and measured risk-taking. Seeking your niche and launching a company are just simple activities. However, careful preparation and intervention are necessary to make this a success. Make sure you don't undersell yourself & that you also stand out.

2.25 Advantage of starting a soap making business at home

Soap making requires little investment to start with

The supplies needed to make soap can be easily acquired

Equipment required can also be easily acquired

It is comparatively much easier to learn the making of soap

There is already good demand for handmade soap and people are willing to purchase handmade soap,

You can easily specialize in your particular field

It's rather easier to make soap that is both distinctive and different from the existing ones

You can create other products that can gel in with your existing products

You can generate handsome profits by selling soap

It is very easy to locate a market for the soaps

2.26 How Much Money Can You Make Making Soap?

That's a tough question to answer because so much depends on you. And, just to be clear, producing soap is not lucrative. Of course, the money is in the soap sales. To make money selling a product, much as with any other business endeavor takes a lot of time and commitment.

CHAPTER 3: Start a Profitable Candle Making Business

Candlemakers are extremely professional artisans who pay particular attention to the sensory aesthetics of their products and experienced business people who know how to entice consumers with innovative marketing tactics. Learn how to launch a candle-making company of your own.

3.1 Steps for starting a candle making business

You've uncovered the ideal market opportunity and are now prepared to take the next step. There's more to launching a company than simply filing papers with the government. We've put together a list of steps to help you get started with your candle-making business. These measures will ensure that the new company is well-planned, legally compliant, and properly registered.

Plan your business

As an entrepreneur, you must have a well-thought-out strategy. It will assist you in figuring out the additional data of your organization and uncovering any unknowns. Given below are some key points to consider:

What are the startup and recurring costs?

Who is the targeted audience?

What is the maximum price you will charge from the customers?

What would you name your company?

What are the costs involved in opening a candle-making business?

You will be able to start your business at home, based on local zoning rules, making use of your kitchen heat source as well as utensils. Many online retailers, including Candle Science and CandleChem, offer a starter kit of items. To start, your candle materials shouldn't cost more than a few hundred dollars. This includes:

Paraffin, gel, soy, beeswax, or other wax

Wicks

Jars, tins, or other containers (though bear in mind that if you're just selling pillar candles, you won't need containers)

Fragrance oils

Coloring agents

Packaging materials

Transportation costs of raw goods in and finished products out

Web growth, which can cost anywhere from nothing to a few hundred dollars based on the expertise in the industry and at least properly contributes to some other start-up costs. A booth will cost $100 per day if you intend to showcase your goods at different exhibits and festivals, plus you'll have to pay for fuel and other travel expenses. You can also contact an insurance provider first. Since there is a chance of a fire accident, you can ensure that your company is fire-proofed and that you have a fire extinguisher onboard. You can also have an initial consultation with a lawyer to decide what licenses or permits are required in your region.

What are the ongoing expenses for a candle-making business?

The majority of the business revolves around different varieties of wax, your containers, and paint and scent additives. You can purchase these goods in bulk at lower per-unit prices once you've established your business model is viable. Wax, for example, can be ordered in 25-pound sizes for as little as a dollar per pound. Wicks are sold in 100-foot spools. Bulk amounts of containers, such as glass pots, mason jars, and tins, are also available.

Who is the target market?

Anyone who needs candles is your end customer. Some may have specific concerns, such as lights in the case of a power outage, and others are searching for a more sensory experience. Churches that use candles to decorate prayer offerings or stores that wish to bring a dramatic effect to their showrooms are often fantastic consumers. You may also approach resellers that can order the goods in vast quantities. Shop owners from the neighborhood and beyond will be among them. Customers like these are usually seen at arts and crafts shows. Try renting stalls at arts and crafts shows, flea markets, festivals and fairs, and other similar venues if you love seeing your customers face to face in an atmosphere where they can truly appreciate the aesthetics of your goods.

How does a candle-making business make money?

Candlemakers market candles to customers directly or indirectly through resellers such as boutiques, gift stores, and other arts and crafts shopping outlets. Since candle making is such a wide field, differentiate yourself by the types of candles you sell (pillar, floating, votive, tea, etc.) or the quality of your offering. Experiment with scents, textures, and molds to come up with something unique that is worth premium pricing. Furthermore, for optimum profit margins on your sales, you can still be on the lookout for low-cost raw material suppliers. To widen your target audience, think of related products or candle styles.

3.2 How much can you charge customers?

Your goods could sell for as little as a few bucks or as much as $20 or more per unit. Pricing will be dictated by the nature and reach of your product line, as well as your target market, marketing plan, and competitiveness. If you want to be the lowest vendor, make sure you're buying your raw materials at a discount and that you're still aware of what your rivals are charging. To save the most cost per unit, you'll want to buy wax, wicks, coloring agents, scents, and other products in bulk. If your goal is to market a higher-end product line, price is less important as long as your goods are visually pleasing. If you find a retail reseller that can move a lot of your product, you might want to consider giving deep discounts on prices.

How much profit can a candle-making business make?

Profit margins of 50% or more are not out of the question. While the cost of materials is not especially high, make sure you have the resources to devote to making your company profitable.

How can you make your business more profitable?

Consider expanding the product offerings once you've perfected the principles of candle-making. For example, learning how to mold or carve candles into any shape will improve the cost and revenue potential. Alternatively, you might start selling fancy oil lamps made from liquid candles. Find scented soaps and incense as well as other sensory items. You might be able to learn how to make these additions to your expanding product line, or you might be able to figure out where to purchase them for resale. Consider offering candle-making lessons if you have the requisite space in your workshop. You might contact the local community center or community college in this effort and see if they'd be involved in adding your class to their program. Finally, is the company prosperous enough that you might consider franchising it? You have to give this important factor a thorough consideration if you want to enhance your profits.

What will you name your business?

Choosing the correct name is vital and daunting. If you own a sole proprietorship, you should start using a separate company name from your own. We suggest reviewing the following references before filing a company name:

The state's business records

Federal and state trademark records

Social media sites

Web domain availability

It's important to get your domain name registered before anyone else. After registering a domain name, you should consider setting up a professional email account (@yourcompany.com).

Form a legal entity

The sole proprietorship, partnership, limited liability company (LLC), and corporation are the most traditional corporate structures. If your candle manufacturing company is used, creating a legitimate business entity such as an LLC or corporation prevents you from being found legally accountable.

Register for taxes

Before you can start doing business, you'll need to apply for several state and federal taxes. You would need to apply for an EIN to pay for taxation. It's very basic and free.

Small Business Taxes

Depending on which business arrangement you select, you can have various taxation choices for your corporation. There could be state-specific taxes that apply to your business. In the state sales tax guides, you can read more about state sales taxes and franchise taxes.

Open a business bank account & credit card

Personal wealth security necessitates the use of dedicated company banking and credit accounts. If your personal and corporate accounts are combined, your personal properties (such as your house, vehicle, and other valuables) are put at risk if your company-issued. This is referred to as piercing the corporate veil in business law. Furthermore, learning how to create company credit will help you receive credit cards and another borrowing under your business's name (rather than your own), lower interest rates, and more credit lines, among other advantages.

Open a business bank account

This protects your assets from those of your business, which is essential for personal wealth security, as well as making accounting and tax reporting simpler.

Get a business credit card

It will help you achieve the following benefits:

It builds the company's credit background and will be beneficial for raising capital and profit later on.

It lets you differentiate personal and business expenditures by placing all of your business's costs under one account.

Set up business accounting

Understanding your business's financial results includes keeping track of your different costs and sources of revenue. Maintaining correct and comprehensive reports also makes annual tax filing even simpler.

Labor safety requirements

It is essential to comply with all Occupational Safety and Health Administration protocols. Pertinent requirements include:

Employee injury report

Safety signage

Certificate of Occupancy

A Certificate of Occupancy is normally required for businesses that operate out of a specific location (CO). All requirements concerning building codes, zoning rules, and local requirements have been followed, according to a CO. If you're thinking about renting a space, keep the following in mind:

Securing a CO is normally the landlord's duty.

Before signing a contract, make sure your landlord has or can get a legitimate CO for a soap-making operation.

A new CO is often needed after a significant renovation. If your company will be renovated before opening, add wording in your lease agreement that specifies that lease payments will not begin before a valid CO is issued.

If you intend to buy or build a place:

You would be responsible for securing a legal CO from a local government body.

Review all building codes and zoning standards for your candle-making business's place to ensure that you'll comply and eligible to get a CO.

Trademark & Copyright Protection

It is wise to protect your interests by applying for the required trademarks and copyrights if you are creating a new product, idea, brand, or design. The essence of legal standards in distance education is continually evolving, especially when it comes to copyright laws. This is a regularly revised database that can assist you with keeping on top of legal specifications.

Get business insurance

Insurance, including licenses and permits, are necessary for your company to run safely and legally. In the case of a covered loss, corporate insurance covers your company's financial well-being. There are several insurance schemes tailored for diverse types of companies with various risks. If you're not sure what kinds of risks your company might face, start with General Liability Insurance.

This is the most popular form of coverage required by small companies, so it's a good place to start.

Define your brand

Your company's brand is what it stands for, as well as how the general public perceives it. A good name would set the company apart from the market.

How to promote & market a candle making business

The first and most crucial step is to decide who you intend to reach. Is your average customer a cost-conscious shopper, or is she more concerned with the sensory experience? If your target market is the former, you should be able to deliver fair prices. If it's the latter, make sure your product range is well-presented and that your color and scent options are pleasing. Try building an online presence on sites including eBay, Amazon, and Etsy. Since these platforms have a lot of competition, keep the costs as low as possible. There is a slew of other arts and crafts marketplaces, but they aren't as well-known as Etsy (and therefore potentially less populated with competitors). Among them are ArtFire, Big Cartel, and Craft Is Art, to name a few.

How to keep customers coming back

You aim to not only retain buyers but to keep them coming back. Since candles are consumable goods that must be replaced daily, the current consumer partnerships may become profitable over time. As a result, make sure you fulfill their needs so that they appreciate the quality of your goods and know-how to reach you if stocks run out. As a consequence, any order must provide easy-to-find contact information, such as your website, email address, or phone number (or all three). As part of the packaging, you could add a business card or sticker with this detail. Make sure shoppers and passers-by alike get your business card when approaching clients in people, such as at art shows or flea markets. Often, get their names and permission to connect them to an email list you give out, maybe before peak candle-buying seasons like the holidays or Mother's Day.

Establish your web presence

Customers can learn more about your business and the goods or services you deliver by visiting your website. One of the most successful ways to build your online presence is through press releases and social media.

Top of Form

Bottom of Form

Is this Business Right For You?

The perfect candle maker is passionate about the craft and has experience in sales and promotion. Candlemakers may start small, with a minimal budget and inventory, in the kitchen and storage room of their home or apartment. Since candles are always thought of as commodity products, you must continually search for ways to brand your line to set yourself apart from the competition. Excellent image photography, a solid web presence, and savvy sales expertise can help you highlight your product line attractively.

What are some skills and experiences that will help you build a successful candle-making business?

The bulk of people get into this business as hobby candle builders. You should appreciate the aesthetics of making candles and related products and have a clear understanding of how to mark your business. You should be familiar with the principles of eCommerce and how to build an online presence. If you sell from a booth at a fair, your display presentation skills are relevant both online (in the quality of your images and written product descriptions) and in physical displays. If you plan to market your product line in person, either to consumers personally or to resellers, personal sales skill is important. You must trust in the goods and be able to convince people to do so as well.

What is the growth potential for a candle-making business?

A good full-time candle maker could earn between $25,000 and $50,000 per year. However, if you sell to a big reseller, you might make more money. Consider franchising your organization once it has become popular enough for others to choose to follow in your footsteps. Candle making is an easy business to launch on your own. However, your ambition likely is to become so well-known that you'll need assistance with crafting, selling, and/or shipping your merchandise. Begin by enlisting the support of friends or family members if required, such as to match seasonal revenue spikes. Don't recruit permanent full-time support once you've been through ample revenue periods to realize that you'll be able to easily reach payroll over the year. Also, contact the accountant to hear about all the hidden expenses.

Candles Pricing

From a business standpoint, you'll need to find out how much you need/want to receive every hour and how many candles you can make in that time. Divide the hourly wage by the number of units (candles) generated to get a figure to add to the basic cost of the supplies used to manufacture each candle until you have these two numbers. Consider the following scenario: You pay $50 on ingredients (not equipment) and can make 20 candles from them. For the supplies, you paid $2.50 per candle. Making candles is a way for you to earn $20 per hour. Since the 20 candles you made took two hours to make, the overall cost is two times $20, or $40. Then you divide $40 by 20 to get a $2 per candle labor rate. When you apply the $2 labor cost to the $2.50 content cost, you get $4.50 per candle. This isn't a great example because you'll need to pay for other expenses like the additional utilities needed to produce the candles and the expense of importing supplies like boilers, pots, and jugs.

How much should you charge for candles?

This is based on the sort of brand you choose to be affiliated with. If you intend to sell bulk candles at a low price, you should expect your company to turn out a huge amount of low-cost candles with a slight but steady profit per candle. Votive candles are cheap and can be ordered for as little as $0.50 each. This approach can be very successful, particularly when several cheap candles are purchased in bulk, resulting in several sales for each customer. The drawback is that you would have to bring in a lot of money to make a big profit. You'll almost definitely need to expand, recruiting someone to help you achieve your broad production goals. Another choice is to create your brand. This means catering to a more discerning public able to pay a premium price for a candle. Some high-end artisanal candles will cost upwards of $200 each. For a brand, you'd have to worry about the packaging theme and what you're encouraging your clients to do with their candles.

3.3 Benefits of candle making business

If you've ever visited a big shopping center, you've probably seen a variety of candle shops. There are whole areas devoted to candles in several major department stores. To give you an example of how strong the candle business is, over 1 million pounds of wax are used to produce candles for the US market alone every year. The candle industry is worth around $2.3 billion a year without additional products such as candlesticks, ceramic pots, and so on. Who makes the most candle purchases? Seasonal holidays account for just 35% of overall sales, making them an outstanding all-year-round investment. Outside of these days, candles are purchased for 65 percent of the year. The most popular motives for buying a candle as a present include a seasonal gift, a housewarming gift, a dinner party gift, a thank you gift, and adult birthday presents. People nowadays believe fragrance to be the most important consideration when buying a candle. Make sure the candles you're thinking of selling have high-quality scents since this can be the difference between success and failure in the candle industry.

Conclusion

In 1969, in a period when India's domestic detergent industry had very few competitors, predominantly multi-national firms, which targeted the affluent of India, Karsanbhai launched Nirma. The detergents were not affordable for most middle-class and poor citizens. Karsanbhai began producing detergent powder in the backyard of his home in Khokra, near Ahmedabad and selling it door to door for Rs 3 per kg, while other brands were charging Rs 13 per kg. Business Standard reported how Karsanbhai came up with a genius idea during the early 1980s, when the Nirma was still struggling with the sales, for drying out market of the goods collecting all the due credits. This was accompanied by a huge ad campaign featuring his daughter singing the iconic Nirma jingle in a white frock. Customers were flocking to markets, only to return empty-handed. Karsanbhai flooded the industry with his goods as the demand for Nirma peaked, leading to huge sales. Nirma's sales peaked that year, making it the most successful detergent, well outselling its closest competitor, Hindustan Unilever's Surf. As Karsanbhai purchased the cement firm LafargeHolcim for 1.4 billion dollars that year, he showed once again that the business appetite is away from over. Mint reported how the deal in Rajasthan and the surrounding area would help Nirma achieve a stronger grip. While a media-shy guy, Karsanbhai, an entrepreneur in the truest sense, has a sharp eye for nation-building. In 1995, he founded the Nirma Institute of Technology, which was followed by the Nirma University of Science and Technology, which was founded in 2003 and is supervised by the Nirma Education and Research Foundation. He initiated the education project Nirmalabs in 2004, aimed at educating and incubating entrepreneurs in India. Karsanbhai Patel received the Padma Shri award in 2010. Just like Nirma, you can also transform your soap and candle-making business into large corporate businesses with the help of your ingenious marketing and creative skills, dedication, perseverance, and unfearfulness of new and challenging situations.

Bubble or Revolution? The Basics of Bitcoin and Blockchain.

The Idiot-Proof Guide to Understand the Crypto Market and Become a Skilled Investor and Trader Starting from Scratch.

By

Amir Lime

Table of Contents

Chapter 1. What Is Bitcoin?

Bitcoin is advanced cash that was made in January 2009. It follows the thoughts set out in a white paper by the strange and pseudonymous Satoshi Nakamoto.The personality of the individual or people who made the innovation is as yet a secret. Bitcoin offers the guarantee of lower exchange charges than conventional online installment instruments, and, not at all like officially sanctioned monetary forms, it is worked by a decentralized position.

Bitcoin is a sort of cryptographic money. There are no physical bitcoins and just adjusts on a public record that everybody has straightforward admittance to. A monstrous measure of processing power checks all bitcoin exchanges. Bitcoins are not given or supported by any banks or governments, nor are individual bitcoins significant as a product. Notwithstanding it not being legitimate delicate, Bitcoin is well known and has set off many other digital forms of money, altogether alluded to as Altcoin. Bitcoin is normally condensed as "BTC."

Understanding Bitcoin

The bitcoin framework is an assortment of PCs (additionally alluded to as "hubs" or "diggers") that all run bitcoin's code and store its blockchain. Allegorically, a blockchain can be considered as an assortment of squares. In each square is an assortment of exchanges. Since every one of the PCs running the blockchain has similar rundown of squares and exchanges and can straightforwardly see these new squares being loaded up with new bitcoin exchanges, nobody can swindle the framework.

Regardless of whether they run a bitcoin "hub" or not, anybody can see these exchanges happening live. To accomplish a scandalous demonstration, a troublemaker would have to work 51% of the registering power that makes up bitcoin. Bitcoin has around 12,000 hubs as of January 2021, and this number is developing, making such an assault very unlikely.

In any case, if an assault were to occur, the bitcoin diggers, individuals who participate in the bitcoin network with their PC, would almost certainly fork to another blockchain putting forth the attempt the agitator set forth to accomplish the assault a waste.

Equilibriums of bitcoin tokens are kept utilizing public and hidden "keys," which are long series of numbers and letters connected through the numerical encryption calculation used to make them. The public key (similar to a financial balance number) fills in as the location distributed to the world and to which others may send bitcoins.

The private key (similar to an ATM PIN) is intended to be a watched secret and simply used to approve Bitcoin transmissions. Bitcoin keys ought not to be mistaken for a bitcoin wallet, a physical or computerized gadget that works with the exchanging of bitcoin and permits clients to follow responsibility for. The expression "wallet" is somewhat deceptive, as bitcoin's decentralized nature implies that it is rarely put away "in" a wallet but instead appropriately on a blockchain.

BITCOIN · DIGITAL · DECENTRALIZED PEER TO PEER

Peer-to-Peer Technology

Bitcoin is one of the main advanced monetary standards to utilize distributed innovation to work with moment installments. The autonomous people and organizations that own the overseeing figuring control and take an interest in the bitcoin network bitcoin "excavators" are accountable for handling the exchanges on the blockchain and are roused by remunerations (the arrival of new bitcoin) and exchange charges paid in bitcoin.

These excavators can be considered as the decentralized authority upholding the validity of the bitcoin network. New bitcoin is delivered to the diggers at a fixed yet intermittently declining rate. There is just 21 million bitcoin that can be mined altogether. As of January 30, 2021, there are around 18,614,806 bitcoin in presence and 2,385,193 bitcoin left to be mined.

Along these lines, bitcoin other digital forms of money work uniquely in contrast to fiat cash; in unified financial frameworks, the cash is delivered at a rate coordinating with the development in merchandise; this framework is proposed to keep up value steadiness. A decentralized framework, as bitcoin, sets the delivery rate early and as per a calculation.

Bitcoin Mining

Bitcoin mining is the interaction by which bitcoins are delivered into dissemination. By and large, mining requires settling computationally troublesome riddles to find another square, which is added to the blockchain.

Bitcoin mining adds and confirms exchange records across the organization. Excavators are compensated with a couple bitcoins; the prize is split each 210,000 squares. The square prize was 50 new bitcoins in 2009. On May 11, 2020, the third splitting happened, bringing the prize for each square revelation down to 6.25 bitcoins.

An assortment of equipment can be utilized to mine bitcoin. Nonetheless, some yield higher prizes than others. Certain CPUs, called Application-Specific Integrated Circuits (ASIC), and further developed handling units, similar to Graphic Processing Units (GPUs), can accomplish more rewards. These intricate mining processors are known as "mining rigs."

One bitcoin is detachable to eight decimal spots (100 millionths of one bitcoin), and this littlest unit is alluded to as a Satoshi if important. On the off chance that the taking interest diggers acknowledge the change, Bitcoin could at last be distinguishable to much more decimal spots.

History of Bitcoin

August 18, 2008

The area name bitcoin.org is enrolled. Today, this space is "WhoisGuard Protected," which means the personality of the individual who enrolled it isn't public data.

October 31, 2008

An individual or gathering utilizing the name Satoshi Nakamoto makes a declaration on The Cryptography Mailing list at metzdowd.com: "I've been chipping away at another electronic money framework that is completely distributed, with no confided in outsider. This now-acclaimed whitepaper distributed on bitcoin.org, named "Bitcoin: A Peer-to-Peer Electronic Cash System," would turn into the Magna Carta for how Bitcoin works today.

January 3, 2009

The principal Bitcoin block is mined Block 0. This progression is otherwise called the "beginning square" and contains the content: "The Times 03/Jan/2009 Chancellor near the very edge of second bailout for banks," maybe as evidence that the square was mined on or after that date, and maybe likewise as significant political commentary.

Jan. 8, 2009

The principal variant of the bitcoin programming is reported on The Cryptography Mailing list.

January 9, 2009

Square 1 is mined, and bitcoin mining begins vigorously.

Who Is Satoshi Nakamoto?

No one understands who made bitcoin, or if nothing else not conclusively. Satoshi Nakamoto is the name related with the individual or social event of people who conveyed the main Bitcoin white paper in 2008 and worked on the primary Bitcoin programming conveyed in 2009. Since that time, various individuals have either declared to be or have been proposed as the certifiable people behind the nom de plume. Regardless, as of January 2021, the certified character (or characters) behind Satoshi stays blurred.

Despite the fact that it is enticing to accept the media's twist that Satoshi Nakamoto is a lone, impractical virtuoso who made Bitcoin out of nowhere, such advancements don't ordinarily occur in a vacuum. Regardless of how unique appearing, all major logical revelations were based on beforehand existing exploration.

There are forerunners to Bitcoin: Adam Back's Hashcash, imagined in 1997,8 and thusly Wei Dai's b-cash, Nick Szabo's touch gold, and Hal Finney's Reusable Proof of Work. The bitcoin whitepaper itself refers to Hashcash and b-cash and different works traversing a few examination fields. Maybe obviously, a considerable lot of the people behind different ventures named above have been estimated to have likewise had a section in making bitcoin.

There are a couple of potential inspirations for bitcoin's creators choosing to stay quiet. One is protection: As bitcoin has acquired in notoriety—turning out to be something of an overall wonder—

Satoshi Nakamoto would almost certainly collect a ton of consideration from the media and governments...

Another explanation could be the potential for bitcoin to cause a significant interruption in the current banking and financial frameworks. On the off chance that bitcoin were to acquire mass selection, the framework could outperform countries' sovereign fiat monetary standards. This danger to existing cash could propel governments to need to make a lawful move against bitcoin's maker.

The other explanation is wellbeing. 32,489 squares were mined; at the award pace of 50 bitcoin per block, the absolute payout in 2009 was 1,624,500 bitcoin. One may reason that solitary Satoshi and maybe a couple of others were mining through 2009 and have a dominant part of that reserve of bitcoin.

Somebody possessing that much bitcoin could turn into an objective of crooks, particularly since bitcoins are less similar to stocks and more like money. The private keys expected to approve spending could be printed out and held under a sleeping pad. The designer of Bitcoin would avoid potential risk to make any blackmail prompted moves discernible; staying mysterious is a decent path for Satoshi to restrict openness.

Special Considerations
Bitcoin as a Form of Payment

Bitcoins can be acknowledged as methods for installment for items sold or benefits gave. Physical stores can show a sign saying "Bitcoin Accepted Here"; the exchanges can be taken care of with the imperative equipment terminal or wallet address through QR codes and contact screen applications. An online business can undoubtedly acknowledge bitcoins by adding this installment alternative to its other online installment choices: Mastercards, PayPal, and so on

Bitcoin Employment Opportunities

The individuals who are independently employed can find paid for a line of work identified with bitcoin. There are a few different ways to accomplish this, for example, making any web access and adding your bitcoin wallet address to the website as a type of installment. There are additionally a few sites and occupation sheets that are committed to computerized monetary standards:

- Cryptogrind unites work searchers and imminent managers through its site.
- Coinality highlights occupations—independent, low maintenance and full-time—that offer installment in bitcoins, just as other digital currencies like Dogecoin and Litecoin
- Jobs4Bitcoins, part of reddit.com
- BitGigs
- Bitwage offers an approach to pick a level of your work check to be changed over into bitcoin and shipped off your bitcoin address.

Putting resources into Bitcoins

Numerous Bitcoin allies accept that advanced cash is what's to come. Numerous people who underwrite bitcoin accept that it works with a lot quicker, low-expense installment framework for exchanges around the world. Albeit any administration or national bank doesn't back it, bitcoin can be traded for conventional monetary forms; truth be told, its conversion scale against the dollar draws in expected financial backers and brokers intrigued by cash plays. For sure, one of the essential purposes behind the development of computerized monetary standards like bitcoin is that they can go about as an option in contrast to public fiat cash and conventional wares like gold.

In March 2014, the IRS expressed that every virtual cash, including bitcoins, would be burdened as property instead of money. Gains or misfortunes from bitcoins held as capital will be acknowledged as capital increases or misfortunes, while bitcoins held as stock will cause normal additions or misfortunes. The offer of bitcoins that you mined or bought from another gathering, or the utilization of bitcoins to pay for merchandise or administrations, is instances of exchanges that can be burdened.

Like some other resource, the standard of purchasing low and selling high applies to bitcoins. The most famous method of storing up the money is through purchasing on a bitcoin trade, however there are numerous alternate approaches to procure and claim bitcoins.

Types of Risks Associated With Bitcoin Investing

In spite of the fact that Bitcoin was not planned as an ordinary value venture (no offers have been given), some theoretical financial backers were attracted to the computerized cash after it appreciated quickly in May 2011 and again in November 2013. Subsequently, numerous individuals buy bitcoin for its speculation esteem as opposed to its capacity to go about as a mode of trade.

Nonetheless, the absence of ensured worth and its advanced nature implies the buy and utilization of bitcoins conveys a few inalienable dangers. Numerous financial backer cautions have been given by the Securities and Exchange Commission (SEC), the Financial Industry Regulatory Authority (FINRA), the Consumer Financial Protection Bureau (CFPB), and different organizations.

The idea of virtual cash is as yet novel and, contrasted with conventional speculations; bitcoin doesn't have a very remarkable longterm history or history of validity to back it. With their expanding prominence, bitcoins are turning out to be fewer tests each day; after just 10 years, all advanced monetary forms stay in an improvement stage. "It is essentially the most noteworthy danger, best yield venture that you can make," says Barry Silbert, CEO of Digital Currency Group, which fabricates and puts resources into Bitcoin and blockchain organizations.

Administrative Risk

Putting cash into bitcoin in any of its numerous pretenses isn't for the danger loath. Bitcoins are an adversary to government cash and might be utilized for underground market exchanges, illegal tax avoidance, criminal operations, or tax avoidance. Therefore, governments may look to manage, confine, or boycott the utilization and offer of bitcoins (and some as of now have). Others are thinking of different standards.

For instance, in 2015, the New York State Department of Financial Services settled guidelines that would require organizations managing the purchase, sell, move, or capacity of bitcoins to record the personality of clients, have a consistence official, and keep up capital stores. The exchanges worth $10,000 or more should be recorded and detailed.

The absence of uniform guidelines about bitcoins (and other virtual money) brings up issues over their life span, liquidity, and all-inclusiveness.

Security Risk

Most people who own and use bitcoin have not procured their tokens through mining activities. Maybe, they purchase and sell bitcoin and other computerized monetary standards on some famous online business sectors, known as bitcoin trades.

Bitcoin trades are completely computerized and, similarly as with any virtual framework, are in danger from programmers, malware, and operational glitches. In the event that a criminal accesses a Bitcoin proprietor's PC hard drive and takes their private encryption key, they could move the taken bitcoin to another record. (Clients can forestall this just if bitcoins are put away on a

PC that isn't associated with the Internet, or, more than likely by deciding to utilize a paper wallet printing out the bitcoin private keys and addresses and not keeping them on a PC by any means.)

Programmers can likewise target Bitcoin trades, accessing a great many records and advanced wallets where bitcoins are put away. One particularly famous hacking episode occurred in 2014, when Mt. Gox, a bitcoin trade in Japan, had to shut down after large number of dollars' worth of bitcoins was taken.

This is especially hazardous, given that all Bitcoin exchanges are lasting and irreversible. It resembles managing cash: Any exchange did with bitcoins must be turned around if the individual who has gotten them discounts them. There is no outsider or an installment processor, as on account of a charge or MasterCard—thus, no wellspring of assurance or allure if there is an issue.

Protection Risk

A few ventures are safeguarded through the Securities Investor Protection Corporation. Typical financial balances are guaranteed through the Federal Deposit Insurance Corporation (FDIC) up to a specific sum contingent upon the purview.

As a rule, bitcoin trades and bitcoin accounts are not protected by any bureaucratic or government program. In 2019, the great seller and exchanging stage SFOX reported it would furnish bitcoin financial backers with FDIC protection, however just for the part of exchanges including cash.13

Extortion Risk

While bitcoin utilizes private key encryption to check proprietors and register exchanges, fraudsters and tricksters may endeavor to sell bogus bitcoins. For example, in July 2013, the SEC brought lawful activity against an administrator of a bitcoin-related Ponzi conspire. There have likewise been recorded instances of bitcoin value control, another basic type of misrepresentation.

Market Risk

Like with any speculation, Bitcoin esteems can vary. Undoubtedly, the money's worth has seen wild swings in cost over its short presence. Subject to high volume purchasing and selling on trades, it has a high affectability to any newsworthy occasions. As per the CFPB, the cost of bitcoins fell by 61% in a solitary day in 2013, while the one-day value drop record in 2014 was just about as large as 80%.

In the event that fewer individuals start to acknowledge bitcoin as money, these computerized units may lose esteem and could get useless. Without a doubt, there was theory that the "bitcoin bubble" had blasted when the cost declined from its untouched high during the cryptographic money surge in late 2017 and mid-2018.

There is as of now a lot of rivalry. In spite of the fact that Bitcoin has a colossal lead over the many other advanced monetary standards that have jumped up on account of its image acknowledgment and investment cash, a mechanical leap forward as a superior virtual coin is consistently a danger.

Splits in the Cryptocurrency Community

In the years since Bitcoin dispatched, there have been various examples in which conflicts between groups of excavators and engineers incited huge scope parts of the digital currency local area. In a portion of these cases, gatherings of Bitcoin clients and diggers have changed the bitcoin network convention itself.

This cycle is known as "forking" and it as a rule brings about making another sort of bitcoin with another name. This split can be a "hard fork," in which another coin imparts exchange history to bitcoin until a definitive split point, so, all in all another token is made. Instances of cryptographic forms of money that have been made because of hard forks incorporate bitcoin cash (made in August 2017), bitcoin gold (made in October 2017), and Bitcoin SV (made in November 2017).

A "delicate fork" is a change to the convention that is as yet viable with the past framework rules. For instance, bitcoin delicate forks have expanded the complete size of squares.

Chapter 2. What is Blockchain?

Blockchain appears to be convoluted, and it unquestionably can be, yet its center idea is very basic. A blockchain is a sort of data set. Understanding blockchain assists first with understanding what an information base is.

A data set is an assortment of data that is put away electronically on a PC framework. In data sets, data or information is regularly organized in table arrangement to take into consideration simpler looking and separating of explicit data. What is the contrast between utilizing a bookkeeping page to store data instead of an information base?

Bookkeeping pages are intended for one individual, or a little gathering of individuals, to store and access restricted measures of data. Conversely, a data set is intended to house altogether bigger measures of data that can be gotten to, separated, and controlled rapidly and effectively by quite a few clients on the double.

Enormous data sets accomplish this by lodging information on workers made of amazing PCs. These workers can some of the time be constructed utilizing hundreds or thousands of PCs to have the computational force and capacity limit important for some clients to get to the information base at the same time. While a bookkeeping page or information base might be open to numerous individuals, it is regularly possessed by a business and overseen by a selected person who has unlimited oversight over how it functions and the information inside it.

Storage Structure

One key distinction between a normal data set and a blockchain is the manner by which the information is organized. A blockchain gathers data together in gatherings, otherwise called blocks that hold sets of data. Squares have certain capacity limits and, when filled, are affixed onto the recently filled square, framing a chain of information known as the "blockchain." All new data that follows that newly added block is arranged into a recently shaped square that will at that point likewise be added to the chain once filled.

A data set designs its information into tables, while a blockchain, similar to its name suggests, structures its information into pieces (blocks) affixed together. This makes it with the goal that all blockchains are data sets, however not all data sets are blockchains. This framework likewise naturally makes an irreversible timetable of information when executed in a decentralized nature. At the point when a square is filled, it is unchangeable and turns into a piece of this course of events. Each square in the chain is given a precise timestamp when added to the chain.

Decentralization

For comprehension blockchain, it is informative to see it with regards to how Bitcoin has carried out it. Like an information base, Bitcoin needs an assortment of PCs to store its blockchain. For Bitcoin, this blockchain is only a particular kind of information base that stores each Bitcoin exchange at any point made. For Bitcoin's situation, and not at all like most information bases, these PCs are not all under one rooftop. Every PC or gathering of PCs is worked by an exceptional individual or gathering of people.

Envision that an organization claims a worker included 10,000 PCs with a data set holding the entirety of its customer's record data. This organization has a stockroom containing these PCs under one rooftop and has full control of every one of these PCs and all the data contained inside them. Likewise, Bitcoin comprises of thousands of PCs. All things considered, every PC or gathering of PCs that hold its blockchain is in an alternate geographic area, and they are completely worked by independent people or gatherings of individuals. These PCs that make up Bitcoin's Network are called hubs.

In this model, Bitcoin's blockchain is utilized in a decentralized way. Nonetheless, private, concentrated blockchains, where the PCs that make up its organization are possessed and worked by a solitary substance, exist.

In a blockchain, every hub has a full record of the information that has been put away on the blockchain since its commencement. For Bitcoin, the information is the whole history of all Bitcoin exchanges. In the event that one hub has a mistake in its information, it can utilize the huge number of different hubs as a kind of perspective highlight right itself. Thusly, nobody hub inside the organization can adjust data held inside it. Along these lines, the historical backdrop of exchanges in each square that make up Bitcoin's blockchain is irreversible.

In the event that one client alters Bitcoin's record of exchanges, any remaining hubs would cross-reference one another and effectively pinpoint the hub with the mistaken data. This framework assists with setting up a definite and straightforward request of occasions. For Bitcoin, this data is a rundown of exchanges. In any case, it is likewise feasible for a blockchain to hold different data like lawful agreements, state distinguishing pieces of proof, or an organization's item stock.

To change how that framework functions or the data put away inside it, the vast majority of the decentralized organization's registering force would have to concur on said changes. This guarantees that whatever changes happen are in the greater part's wellbeing.

Transparency

On account of the decentralized idea of Bitcoin's blockchain, everything exchanges can be straightforwardly seen by either having an individual hub or by utilizing blockchain wayfarer that permits anybody to see exchanges happening live. Every hub has its duplicate of the chain that gets refreshed as new squares are affirmed and added. This implies that you could follow Bitcoin any place it goes in the event that you needed to.

For instance, trades have been hacked in the past were the individuals who held Bitcoin on the trade lost everything. While the programmer might be altogether unknown, the Bitcoins they separated are effectively detectable. On the off chance that the Bitcoins taken in a portion of these hacks were to be moved or spent some place, it would be known.

Is Blockchain Secure?

Blockchain innovation represents the issues of safety and trust severally. To start with, new squares are constantly put away directly and sequentially. They are constantly added to the "end" of the blockchain. In the event that you take a gander at Bitcoin's blockchain, you'll see that each square has a situation on the chain, called a "tallness." As of November 2020, the square's stature had arrived at 656,197 squares up until now.

After a square has been added to the furthest limit of the blockchain, it is hard to return and change the substance of the square except if the larger part arrived at an agreement to do as such. That is on the grounds that each square contains its hash, alongside the hash of the square before it, just as the recently referenced time stamp. Hash codes are made by a numerical capacity that transforms advanced data into a series of numbers and letters. On the off chance that that data is altered in any capacity, the hash code changes.

Here's the reason that is critical to security. Suppose a programmer needs to modify the blockchain and take Bitcoin from every other person. If they somehow happened to change their single duplicate, it would presently don't line up with every other person's duplicate. At the point when every other person cross-references their duplicates against one another, they would see this one duplicate stick out, and that programmer's rendition of the chain would be given away a role as ill-conceived.

Prevailing with such a hack would necessitate that the programmer at the same time control and change 51% of the duplicates of the blockchain so their new duplicate turns into the dominant part duplicate and, along these lines, the settled upon chain. Such an assault would likewise require a tremendous measure of cash and assets as they would have to re-try the entirety of the squares since they would now have distinctive timestamps and hash codes.

Because of the size of Bitcoin's Network and how quick it is developing, the expense to pull off such an accomplishment would most likely be inconceivable. In addition to the fact that this would be amazingly costly, yet it would likewise likely be vain. Doing something like this would not go undetected, as organization individuals would see such radical changes to the blockchain. The organization individuals would then fork off to another rendition of the chain that has not been influenced.

This would make the assaulted form of Bitcoin fall in esteem, making the assault at last trivial as the troublemaker controls a useless resource. The equivalent would happen if the agitator assaulted the new fork of Bitcoin. It is constructed this way so that participating in the organization is definitely more financially boosted than assaulting it.

Bitcoin vs. Blockchain

The objective of blockchain is to permit advanced data to be recorded and appropriated yet not altered. Blockchain innovation was first laid out in 1991 by Stuart Haber and W. Scott Stornetta, two analysts who needed to carry out a framework where archive timestamps couldn't be messed with. In any case, it wasn't until right around twenty years after the fact, with the dispatch of Bitcoin in January 2009, that blockchain had its first genuine application.

The Bitcoin convention is based on a blockchain. In an exploration paper presenting the computerized money, Bitcoin's pseudonymous maker, Satoshi Nakamoto, alluded to it as "another electronic money framework that is completely shared, with no confided in outsider."

The critical thing to comprehend here is that Bitcoin simply utilizes blockchain to record a record of installments straightforwardly. In any case, in principle, blockchain can be utilized to record quite a few information focuses changelessly. As talked about over, this could be as exchanges, votes in a political decision, item inventories, state IDs, deeds to homes, and considerably more.

There is a wide assortment of blockchain-based activities hoping to carry out blockchain in approaches to help society other than recording exchanges. One genuine model is that of blockchain being utilized to cast a ballot in just decisions. The idea of blockchain's changelessness implies that deceitful democratic would get undeniably harder to happen.

For instance, a democratic framework could work to such an extent that every resident of a nation would be given a solitary digital currency or token. Every competitor would then be given a particular wallet address, and the electors would send their token or crypto to whichever up-and-comer's location they wish to decide in favor of. The straightforward and recognizable nature of blockchain would take out the requirement for human vote checking and the capacity of agitators to mess with actual polling forms.

Blockchain versus Banks

Banks and decentralized blockchains are inconceivably extraordinary. To perceive how a bank contrasts from blockchain, we should contrast the financial framework with Bitcoin's blockchain execution.

How is Blockchain Used?

As we currently know, blocks on Bitcoin's blockchain store information about money related exchanges. Yet, incidentally, blockchain is a solid method of putting away information about different sorts of exchanges.

A few organizations that have effectively joined blockchain incorporate Wal-Mart, Pfizer, AIG, Siemens, Unilever, and a large group of others. For instance, IBM has made its Food Trust blockchain to follow the excursion that food items take to get to their areas.

For what reason do this? The food business has seen endless flare-ups of e Coli, salmonella, listeria, and unsafe materials being unintentionally acquainted with food varieties. It has required a long time to discover the wellspring of these episodes or the reason for infection from what individuals are eating before.

Utilizing blockchain enables brands to follow a food item's course from its root, through each stop it makes, lastly, it is conveyance. In the event that a food is discovered to be sullied, it very well may be followed back through each stop to its root. That, however these organizations can likewise now see all the other things they may have interacted with, permitting the recognizable proof of the issue to happen far sooner, conceivably saving lives. This is one illustration of blockchains practically speaking yet numerous other blockchain execution structures.

Banking and Finance

Maybe no industry stands to profit by coordinating blockchain into its business activities more than banking. Monetary foundations just work during business hours, five days every week. That implies in the event that you attempt to store a keep an eye on Friday at 6 p.m., you will probably need to stand by until Monday morning to see that cash hit your record. Regardless of whether you set aside your installment during business hours, the exchange can in any case take one to three days to check because of the sheer volume of exchanges that banks need to settle. Blockchain, then again, never dozes.

By coordinating blockchain into banks, shoppers can see their exchanges prepared in just 10 minutes. The time it takes to add a square to the blockchain, paying little heed to occasions or the hour of day or week. With blockchain, banks additionally can trade assets between establishments all the more rapidly and safely. For instance, in the stock exchanging business, the repayment and clearing cycle can require as long as three days (or more, if exchanging universally), implying that the cash and offers are frozen for that period.

Given the size of the whole in question, even the couple of days that the cash is on the way can convey significant expenses and dangers for banks. European bank Santander and its exploration accomplices put the possible investment funds at $15 billion to $20 billion per year. Cap Gemini, a French consultancy, appraises that buyers could set aside to $16 billion in banking and protection charges every year through blockchain-based applications.

Money

Blockchain structures the bedrock for digital currencies like Bitcoin. The Federal Reserve controls the US dollar. Under this focal power framework, a client's information and money are in fact at the impulse of their bank or government. In the event that a client's bank is hacked, the customer's private data is in danger. On the off chance that the customer's bank breakdowns or they live in a country with a precarious government, the worth of their money might be in danger. In 2008, a portion of the banks that ran out of cash were rescued in part utilizing citizen cash. These are the concerns out of which Bitcoin was first imagined and created.

By spreading its activities across an organization of PCs, blockchain permits Bitcoin and other digital currencies to work without the requirement for a focal power. This lessens hazard and disposes of a large number of the preparing and exchange expenses. It can likewise give those in nations with insecure monetary standards or monetary frameworks a more steady cash with more applications and a more extensive organization of people and establishments they can work with, both locally and universally.

Utilizing digital money wallets for investment accounts or as methods for installment is particularly significant for the individuals who have no state recognizable proof. A few nations might be war-torn or have governments that do not have any genuine foundation to give ID. Such nations might not approach reserve funds or money market funds and, hence, no real way to store abundance securely.

Medical care

Medical care suppliers can use blockchain to store their patients' clinical records safely. At the point when a clinical record is created and marked, it tends to be composed into the blockchain, which gives patients the evidence and certainty that the record can't be changed. These individual wellbeing records could be encoded and put away on the blockchain with a private key so they are just open by specific people, accordingly guaranteeing security.

Records of Property

On the off chance that you have at any point invested energy in your nearby Recorder's Office, you will realize that the way toward recording property rights is both difficult and wasteful. Today, an actual deed should be conveyed to an administration representative at the neighborhood recording office, where it is physically gone into the region's focal data set and general list. On account of a property debate, cases to the property should be accommodated with the overall file.

This interaction isn't simply expensive and tedious; it is additionally filled with human mistake, where every error makes following property proprietorship less productive. Blockchain can possibly kill the requirement for filtering archives and finding actual documents in a nearby account office. On the off chance that property proprietorship is put away and checked on the blockchain, proprietors can believe that their deed is precise and forever recorded.

In war-torn nations or zones with practically zero government or monetary foundation and absolutely no "Recorder's Office," it very well may be almost difficult to demonstrate responsibility for property. On the off chance that a gathering of individuals living in such a region can use blockchain, straightforward and clear timetables of land owners could be set up.

Shrewd Contract

A savvy contract is a PC code incorporated into the blockchain to work with, confirm, or arrange an agreement understanding. Savvy contracts work under a bunch of conditions that clients consent to. At the point when those conditions are met, the provisions of the understanding are naturally done.

Say, for instance, a potential occupant might want to rent a loft utilizing a keen agreement. The landowner consents to give the inhabitant the entryway code to the condo when the occupant pays the security store. Both the inhabitant and the property manager would send their particular bits of the arrangement to the savvy contract, which would clutch and naturally trade the entryway code for the security store on the date the rent starts. On the off chance that the property manager doesn't supply the entryway code by the rent date, the shrewd agreement discounts the security store. This would wipe out the expenses and cycles normally connected with utilizing a legal official, outsider arbiter, or lawyers.

Supply Chains

As in the IBM Food Trust model, providers can utilize blockchain to record the roots of their bought materials. This would permit organizations to confirm the credibility of their items, alongside such basic marks as "Natural," "Neighborhood," and "Reasonable Trade."

As revealed by Forbes, the food business is progressively receiving blockchain to follow the way and security of food all through the homestead to-client venture.

Casting a ballot

As referenced, blockchain could be utilized to work with a cutting edge casting a ballot framework. Casting a ballot with blockchain conveys the possibility to wipe out political race misrepresentation and lift elector turnout, as was tried in the November 2018 midterm decisions in West Virginia. Utilizing blockchain in this manner would make cast a ballot almost difficult to alter. The blockchain convention would likewise keep up straightforwardness in the appointive interaction, lessening the faculty expected to lead a political decision and giving authorities almost moment results. This would dispose of the requirement for describes or any genuine worry that misrepresentation may compromise the political race.

Advantages and Disadvantages of Blockchain

For the entirety of its intricacy, blockchain's potential as a decentralized type of record-keeping is practically limitless. From more prominent client protection and increased security to bring down preparing expenses and less mistakes, blockchain innovation may well see applications past those laid out above. However, there are additionally a few burdens.

Pros

- Improved exactness by eliminating human contribution in check
- Cost decreases by disposing of outsider check
- Decentralization makes it harder to mess with
- Transactions are secure, private, and effective
- Transparent innovation
- Provides a financial other option and approach to protect individual data for residents of nations with precarious or immature governments

Cons

- Significant innovation cost related with mining bitcoin
- Low exchanges each second
- History of utilization in unlawful exercises
- Regulation

Here are the selling points of blockchain for organizations available today in more detail.

S

Benefits of Blockchain

Exactness of the Chain

An organization endorses exchanges on the blockchain organization of thousands of PCs. This eliminates practically all human inclusion in the check cycle, bringing about less human blunder and an exact record of data. Regardless of whether a PC on the organization were to commit a computational error, the blunder would just be made to one duplicate of the blockchain. For that mistake to spread to the remainder of the blockchain, at any rate 51% of the organization's PCs would should be made—a close to difficulty for an enormous and developing organization the size of Bitcoin's.

Cost Reductions

Ordinarily, buyers pay a bank to confirm an exchange, a public accountant to sign a record, or a priest to play out a marriage. Blockchain wipes out the requirement for outsider confirmation and, with it, their related expenses. Entrepreneurs cause a little expense at whatever point they acknowledge installments utilizing Visas, for instance, since banks and installment preparing organizations need to deal with those exchanges. Then again, Bitcoin doesn't have a focal position and has restricted exchange charges.

Decentralization

Blockchain doesn't store any of its data in a focal area. All things being equal, the blockchain is replicated and spread across an organization of PCs. At whatever point another square is added to the blockchain, each PC on the organization refreshes its blockchain to mirror the change. By spreading that data across an organization, blockchain turns out to be harder to mess with as opposed to putting away it in one focal data set. In the event that a duplicate of the blockchain fell under the control of a programmer, just a solitary duplicate of the data, as opposed to the whole organization, would be undermined.

Productive Transactions

Exchanges put through a focal authority can take up to a couple of days to settle. On the off chance that you endeavor to store a mind Friday evening, for instance, you may not see assets in your record until Monday morning. While monetary establishments work during business hours, five days every week, blockchain is working 24 hours per day, seven days per week, and 365 days per year. Exchanges can be finished in just ten minutes and can be viewed as secure after only a couple hours. This is especially valuable for cross-line exchanges, which generally take any longer on account of time-region issues and that all gatherings should affirm installment preparing.

Private Transactions

Numerous blockchain networks work as open information bases, implying that anybody with a web association can see an organization's exchange history list. Despite the fact that clients can get to insights regarding exchanges, they can't get to recognizing data about the clients making those exchanges. It is a typical misperception that blockchain networks like bitcoin are unknown when they are just secret.

At the point when a client unveils exchanges, their special code called a public key is recorded on the blockchain as opposed to their own data. In the event that an individual has made a Bitcoin buy on a trade that requires recognizable proof, at that point the individual's character is as yet connected to their blockchain address. In any case, in any event, when attached to an individual's name, an exchange doesn't uncover any close to home data.

Secure Transactions

When an exchange is recorded, its credibility should be checked by the blockchain network. A great many PCs on the blockchain hurry to affirm that the buy subtleties are right. After a PC has approved the exchange, it is added to the blockchain block. Each square on the blockchain contains its exceptional hash, alongside the novel hash of the square before it. At the point when the data on a square is altered in any capacity, that square's hash code changes; nonetheless, the hash code on the square after it would not. This inconsistency makes it incredibly hard for data on the blockchain to be changed without notice.

Straightforwardness

Most blockchains are altogether open-source programming. This implies that anybody and everybody can see its code. This enables inspectors to audit digital forms of money like Bitcoin for security. This additionally implies no genuine expert on who controls Bitcoin's code or how it is altered. Along these lines, anybody can recommend changes or moves up to the framework. In the event that most organization clients concur that the new form of the code with the overhaul is sound and beneficial, at that point Bitcoin can be refreshed.

Banking the Unbanked

Maybe the most significant aspect of blockchain and Bitcoin is the capacity for anybody, paying little heed to nationality, sex, or social foundation, to utilize it. As indicated by the World Bank, almost 2 billion grown-ups don't have ledgers or any methods for putting away their cash or abundance. Virtually these people live in non-industrial nations where the economy is outset and totally reliant upon cash.

These individuals frequently bring in little cash that is paid in actual money. They at that point need to store this actual money in secret areas in their homes or places of living, leaving them subject to burglary or superfluous viciousness. Keys in a bitcoin wallet can be put away on a piece of paper, a modest cell, or even remembered whether essential. For a great many people likely, these alternatives are more effortlessly covered up than a little heap of money under a sleeping pad.

Blockchains of things to come are likewise searching for answers for be a unit of record for abundance stockpiling and store clinical records, property rights, and an assortment of other legitimate agreements.

Disadvantages of Blockchain

While there are huge potential gains to the blockchain, there are additionally critical difficulties to its appropriation. The barricades to the utilization of blockchain innovation today are not simply specialized. The genuine difficulties are political and administrative, generally, to avoid mentioning the great many hours (read: cash) of custom programming plan and back-end programming needed to coordinate blockchain into current business organizations. Here are a portion of the difficulties holding up traffic of far reaching blockchain appropriation.

Innovation Cost

Despite the fact that blockchain can get a good deal on exchange charges, the innovation is a long way from free. The "evidence of work" framework that bitcoin uses to approve exchanges, for instance, burns-through huge measures of computational force. In reality, the force from the large numbers of PCs on the bitcoin network is near what Denmark burns-through yearly. Accepting power expenses of \$0.03~\$0.05 each kilowatt-hour, mining costs elite of equipment costs are about \$5,000~\$7,000 per coin.

In spite of the expenses of mining bitcoin, clients keep on driving up their power bills to approve exchanges on the blockchain. That is on the grounds that when diggers add a square to the bitcoin blockchain, they are remunerated with enough bitcoin to make their time and energy advantageous. In any case, with regards to blockchains that don't utilize cryptographic money, excavators should be paid or in any case boosted to approve exchanges.

A few answers for these issues are starting to emerge. For instance, bitcoin mining ranches have been set up to utilize sun oriented force, overabundance petroleum gas from deep oil drilling destinations, or force from wind ranches.

Speed Inefficiency

Bitcoin is an ideal contextual analysis for the potential failures of blockchain. Bitcoin's "confirmation of work" framework requires around ten minutes to add another square to the blockchain. At that rate, it's assessed that the blockchain organization can just oversee around seven exchanges each second (TPS). Albeit other digital currencies, for example, Ethereum perform better compared to bitcoin, they are as yet restricted by blockchain. Inheritance brand Visa, for setting, can deal with 24,000 TPS.

Answers for this issue have been being developed for quite a long time. There are presently blockchains that are gloating more than 30,000 exchanges each second.

Criminal behavior

While classification on the blockchain network shields clients from hacks and jelly protection, it additionally takes into account illicit exchanging and movement on the blockchain network. The most referred to illustration of blockchain being utilized for illegal exchanges is likely the Silk Road, an online "dim web" drug commercial center working from February 2011 until October 2013, when the FBI shut it down.

The site permitted clients to peruse the site without being followed utilizing the Tor program and make illicit buys in Bitcoin or other cryptographic forms of money. Current U.S. guidelines require monetary specialist co-ops to acquire data about their clients when they open a record, check the character of every client, and affirm that clients don't show up on any rundown of known or suspected psychological militant associations. This framework can be viewed as both an expert and a con. It gives anybody admittance to monetary records and permits hoodlums to execute all the more without any problem. Many have contended that the great employments of crypto, such as banking the unbanked world, exceed the awful employments of cryptographic money, particularly when most criminal behavior is as yet achieved through untraceable money.

Guideline

Numerous in the crypto space have communicated worries about unofficial law over cryptographic forms of money. While it is getting progressively troublesome and close to difficult to end something like Bitcoin as its decentralized organization develops, governments could hypothetically make it illicit to claim digital currencies or partake in their organizations.

Over the long run this worry has developed more modest as enormous organizations like PayPal start to permit the possession and utilization of cryptographic forms of money on their foundation.

What's Next for Blockchain?

First proposed as an examination project in 1991, blockchain is serenely sinking into its late twenties. Like most recent college grads its age, blockchain has seen something reasonable of public examination in the course of the most recent twenty years, with organizations overall hypothesizing about what the innovation is able to do and where it's going in the years to come.

With numerous commonsense applications for the innovation previously being carried out and investigated, blockchain at long last becomes well known at age 27, in no little part in view of bitcoin and cryptographic money. As a popular expression on the tongue of each financial backer in the country, blockchain stands to make business and government activities more precise, productive, secure, and modest with fewer delegates.

As we get ready to head into the third decade of blockchain, it's not, at this point an issue of "if" heritage organizations will get on to the innovation; it's an issue of "when."

Chapter 3. Understanding the Crypto Market

There are a few things that each trying Bitcoin financial backer necessities. A digital currency trade account, individual ID reports on the off chance that you are utilizing a Know Your Customer (KYC) stage, a safe association with the Internet, and an installment strategy. It is additionally suggested that you have your wallet outside of the trade account. Legitimate techniques for installment utilizing this way incorporate ledgers, charge cards, and Mastercards. It is likewise conceivable to get Bitcoin at particular ATMs and by means of P2P trades. Notwithstanding, know that Bitcoin ATMs progressively required government provided IDs as of mid-2020.

Protection and security are significant issues for Bitcoin financial backers. Despite the fact that there are no actual Bitcoins, it is normally an impractical notion to gloat about enormous possessions. Any individual who acquires the private key to a public location on the Bitcoin blockchain can approve exchanges. Private keys ought to be kept mystery; hoodlums may endeavor to take them on the off chance that they learn huge possessions. Know that anybody can see the equilibrium of a public location you use. That makes it a smart thought to keep critical speculations at public tends to that are not straightforwardly associated with ones that are utilized for exchanges.

Anybody can see a past filled with exchanges made on the blockchain, even you. Yet, while exchanges are openly recorded on the blockchain, distinguishing client data isn't. Just a client's public key shows up close to an exchange on the Bitcoin blockchain, making exchanges secret yet not unknown. One might say, Bitcoin exchanges are more straightforward and detectable than cash; however the cryptographic money can likewise be utilized namelessly.

Following are a few stages you need to follow in the event that you need to put resources into digital currency:

1. Choose an Exchange

Pursuing a digital money trade will permit you to purchase, sell, and hold digital money. It is by and large best practice to utilize a trade that permits clients to likewise pull out their crypto to their online wallet for more secure keeping. This element may not make any difference for those hoping to exchange Bitcoin or other digital forms of money.

There are numerous kinds of digital money trades. Since the Bitcoin ethos is about decentralization and individual sway, a few trades permit clients to stay unknown and don't expect clients to enter individual data. Such trades work self-governing and, commonly, are decentralized, which implies they don't have an essential issue of control.

While such frameworks can be utilized for odious exercises, they are additionally used to offer types of assistance for the world's unbanked populace. For specific classes of individuals - displaced people or those living in nations with practically no administration credit or banking framework - unknown trades can help carry them into the standard economy.

Be that as it may, the most mainstream trades are not decentralized and do require KYC. In the United States, these trades incorporate Coinbase, Kraken, Gemini, and Binance U.S., to give some examples. These trades have filled altogether in the quantity of highlights they offer.

Coinbase, Kraken, and Gemini offer Bitcoin and a developing number of altcoins. These three are presumably the simplest entrance to crypto in the whole business. Binance takes into account a further developed broker, offering more genuine exchanging usefulness and a superior assortment of altcoins to browse.

Something critical to note while making a digital currency trade account is to utilize safe web rehearses. This incorporates utilizing two-factor confirmation and utilizing an extraordinary and long secret phrase, including an assortment of lower-case letters, uppercase letters, exceptional characters, and numbers.

2. Connect Your Exchange to a Payment Option

Whenever you have picked a trade, you presently need to accumulate your reports. Contingent upon the trade, these may incorporate photos of a driver's permit, government managed retirement number, just as data about your boss and wellspring of assets. The data you may need can rely upon the area you live in and its laws. The cycle is to a great extent equivalent to setting up an average investment fund.

After the trade has guaranteed your character and authenticity, you may now interface an installment alternative. At most trades, you can associate your ledger straightforwardly, or you can interface with a charge or Mastercard. While you can utilize a Visa to buy cryptographic money, it is by and large something that ought to be kept away from because of the instability that digital currencies can insight.

While Bitcoin is legitimate in the United States, a few banks don't take excessively benevolent to the thought and may address or even stop stores to crypto-related locales or trades. It is a smart thought to check to guarantee that your bank permits stores at your picked trade.

There are differing expenses for stores by means of a financial balance, charge, or Visa. Coinbase is a strong trade for fledglings and has a 1.49% expense for ledgers, with a 3.99% charge for charge and Mastercards. It is critical to investigate the charges related with every installment choice to help pick a trade or pick which installment alternative works best.

Trades additionally charge expenses per exchange. This charge can either be a level expense (if the exchanging sum is low) or a level of the exchanging sum. Visas cause a handling charge notwithstanding the exchange expenses.

3. Place an Order

Whenever you have picked trade and associated an installment alternative, you would now be able to purchase Bitcoin and other digital forms of money. Lately, cryptographic money trades have gradually become standard. They have filled altogether regarding liquidity and their broadness of highlights. The operational changes at cryptographic money trades equal the adjustment of impression of digital currencies. An industry that was once considered as a trick or one with problematic practices is gradually transforming into a genuine one that has attracted interest from every one of the enormous players the monetary administrations industry.

Presently, cryptographic money trades have arrived at a point where they have almost similar degree of highlights as their stock financier partners. Whenever you have discovered a trade and associated an installment strategy, you are all set.

Crypto trades today offer a few request types and approaches to contribute. Practically all crypto trades offer both market and breaking point requests, and some likewise offer stop-misfortune orders. Of the trades referenced above, Kraken offers the most request types. Kraken takes into account, as far as possible, stop-misfortune, stop-limit, take-benefit, and take-benefit limit orders.

Beside different request types, trades likewise offer approaches to set up repeating speculations permitting customers to dollar cost normal into their ventures of decision. Coinbase, for instance, allows clients to set repeating buys for consistently, week, or month.

4. Safe Storage

Bitcoin and cryptographic money wallets are a spot to store computerized resources all the more safely. Having your crypto outside of the trade and in your wallet guarantees that lone you have authority over the private key to your assets. It additionally enables you to store finances from a trade and keep away from the danger of your trade getting hacked and losing your assets.

A few wallets have a larger number of highlights than others. Some are Bitcoin just, and some offer the capacity to store various altcoins. A few wallets likewise offer the capacity to trade one token for another.

With regards to picking a Bitcoin wallet, you have a few choices. The main thing you should comprehend about crypto wallets is hot wallets (online wallets) and cold wallets (paper or equipment wallets).

5. Hot Wallets

Online wallets are otherwise called "hot" wallets. Hot wallets will be wallets that sudden spike in demand for web associated gadgets like PCs, telephones, or tablets. This can make weakness in light of the fact that these wallets produce the private keys to your coins on these web associated gadgets. While a hot wallet can be advantageous in the manner you can access and make exchanges with your resources rapidly, putting away your private key on a web associated gadget makes it more helpless to a hack.

This may sound unrealistic; however individuals who are not utilizing sufficient security when utilizing these hot wallets can have their assets taken. This is certainly not an inconsistent event, and it can happen by one way or another. For instance, gloating on a public discussion like Reddit about the amount Bitcoin you hold while you are utilizing almost no security and putting away it in a hot wallet would not be savvy. All things considered, these wallets can be made to be secure insofar as insurances are taken. Solid passwords, two-factor verification, and safe web perusing ought to be viewed as least prerequisites.

These wallets are best utilized for modest quantities of digital currency or cryptographic money that you are effectively exchanging on a trade. You could compare a hot wallet to a financial records. Ordinary monetary shrewdness would say to hold just going through cash in a financial records while the heft of your cash is in bank accounts or other speculation accounts. The equivalent could be said for hot wallets. Hot wallets incorporate versatile, work area, web, and trade account guardianship wallets.

As referenced beforehand, trade wallets are custodial records given by the trade. The client of this wallet type isn't the private key holder to the digital currency held in this wallet. On the off chance that an occasion was to happen where the trade is hacked, or your record becomes bargained, your assets would be lost. The expression "not your key, not your coin" is intensely rehashed inside digital money gatherings and networks.

6. Cold Wallets

The easiest portrayal of a cool wallet is a wallet that isn't associated with the Internet and stands at a far lesser danger of being undermined. These wallets can likewise be alluded to as disconnected wallets or equipment wallets.

These wallets store a client's private key on something that isn't associated with the Internet and can accompany programming that works in equal so the client can see their portfolio without putting their private key in danger.

Maybe the most secure approach to store cryptographic money disconnected is by means of a paper wallet. A paper wallet is a wallet that you can create off specific sites. It at that point produces both public and private keys that you print out on a piece of paper. Getting to digital money in these locations is just conceivable in the event that you have that piece of paper with the private key. Numerous individuals cover these paper wallets and store them in wellbeing store boxes at their bank or even protected in their homes. These wallets are intended for high security and long haul ventures since you can't rapidly sell or exchange Bitcoin put away thusly.

An all the more generally utilized kind of chilly wallet is an equipment wallet. An equipment wallet is normally a USB drive gadget that stores a client's private keys safely disconnected. Such wallets have genuine benefits over hot wallets as they are unaffected by infections on one's PC. Private keys never interact with your organization associated PC or possibly weak programming with equipment wallets. These gadgets are likewise normally open-source, permitting the local area to decide its wellbeing through code reviews as opposed to an organization announcing that it is protected to utilize.

Cold wallets are the most secure approach to store your Bitcoin or other cryptographic forms of money. Generally, be that as it may, they require somewhat more information to set up.

Chapter 4. Investing in Crypto Market

Putting resources into cryptographic money has advanced a ton since the pinnacle of 2017, when anybody could rapidly bounce in, get some Bitcoin on their nearby trade, and make a benefit. What the market has instructed us is actually similar to the financial exchange, a more key and thoroughly examined approach should be taken. This eBook contains the nuts and bolts of beginning in this market for the individuals who have no past experience putting resources into cryptographic forms of money. The part that follows, "The One Strategy," that anybody can apply to take their crypto contributing to the following level.

1. Safety First

Before you jump online to begin constructing your pinnacle of crypto power, we should ensure your establishment is strong. This implies that before you start exchanging, your PC, apparatuses, and association should all be just about as free from any and all harm as could really be expected. In the crypto world, there is no bank to run crying to in the event that somebody takes your charge card and purchases 1000 dollars of treats. On the off chance that you get hacked, and your coins are taken, they are GONE. So offer yourself a tremendous kindness and find the accompanying ways to get your venture cash.

Secure Device

A simple spot to begin is to ensure you are utilizing a PC that is tidy and has forward-thinking security programming introduced. Preferably, it's likewise acceptable to exchange from a gadget exclusively utilized for crypto and not one that you additionally use to ride every one of the dull corners of the Internet. Secure organization As hip as it very well may be to purchase Ethereum from your smooth PC in your nearby coffeehouse with an almond milk latte in your grasp, don't exchange utilizing a public organization. No libraries, no eateries, and no malevolent companions' homes. Utilize your organization that is set up to be scrambled and secure.

Great Password Habits

An apparatus we firmly suggest is a secret key supervisor. You've likely caught wind of how significant a solid secret phrase is for limiting your danger of getting hacked (at least fifteen characters, including upper and lower-case letters, numbers, distinctive accentuation marks, and so forth) however, you actually use "timmy123" for the entirety of your records. We get it- - how are you going to recall each one of those diverse convoluted passwords? A secret key director is a piece of programming you can download that allows you to deal with every one of your passwords effectively and successfully, and you can get a beautiful darn great one free of charge

2. Fiat to Crypto

You've currently done, at any rate, what we've requested that you do to put resources into crypto with some degree of safety (perhaps somewhat more since you're that committed to the wellbeing of your future resources.) Now you're prepared to get rolling...

Register at an Exchange

To begin transforming your money into Bitcoin or some other coin (otherwise known as Altcoin), you need to set up a record on a trade. CoinBase is presumably the most notable, yet there are a couple of others, all of which offer fluctuated charge designs and coin contributions. Joining incorporates making a record with various layers of safety and interfacing an installment strategy, which are all clarified bit by bit in the trade's arrangement cycle. Whenever you are done, you are allowed to buy Bitcoin and a few other "fundamental" altcoins, including Ethereum, Bitcoin Cash, and Litecoin.

3. Buying Different Coins

In the event that you will probably go farther than purchase and hold a portion of the principle coins, you'll need to get familiar with purchasing altcoins. Albeit new coins and organizations are promising incredible computerized arrangements springing up consistently, most won't ever proceed to become wildly successful. However, in case you're one of the first to contribute, easily, in another coin that succeeds, you could wind up winning the big stake. To purchase altcoins, you first need to discover which trades offer the Altcoin you might want to put resources into.

Enlisting at one of these trades will be basically the same as the enrollment cycle for your underlying trade. On the off chance that you did it the first occasion when, I have confidence that you can do it a second.

When set up, you should move crypto from your first trade to your new trade. This can be perhaps the most difficult advances in the event that you have never done anything identified with crypto. Basically, this is finished by reordering a location or code for the area you will send your assets to. For a nitty gritty model, we will utilize the guidelines for moving cash out of CoinBase.

Web

- Navigate to the "accounts" interface on the fundamental route bar.
- Select the "send" button for the computerized cash wallet that you'd prefer to send from.

- In the send discourse, select "wallet address" in case you're shipping off a computerized cash wallet outside to CoinBase or "email address" in case you're sending through email.
- Enter the measure of advanced money you'd prefer to send in the "sum" field.
- Alternatively, you can determine the sum you might want to send in your nearby money. Note that the finances will consistently be sent as advanced money, not your nearby cash.
- Click "proceed".
- Confirm the subtleties of the exchange and complete the send.

iOS (For CoinBase portable application)

- Tap the menu symbol close to the upper left of the screen to open the Navbar.
- Select the wallet you wish to send from, situated in the Navbar.
- Tap the paper plane symbol in the upper right hand of the screen.
- Enter the sum you wish to send
- Tap the up/down bolts to switch between monetary forms. • Press "send."
- Enter the email or wallet address and any notes you wish to incorporate.
- Review the subtleties of your exchange and select "send" in the upper right corner of the screen.
-

On the off chance that you have been given a QR code

- Tap the QR symbol in the upper right.
- Take an image of the QR code
- Enter the ideal sum and press "proceed."
- Review the subtleties of your exchange and select "send" in the upper right corner of the screen. Android (For the CoinBase versatile application)
- Tap the menu symbol close to the upper left of the screen to open the Navbar.
- Select the wallet you wish to send from, situated in the Navbar.
- Tap the "+" symbol close to the lower right hand of the screen.
- Select "send."
- Enter the sum you wish to send.
- Use the up/down bolts to switch between kinds of money.
- Enter the email or wallet address and any notes you wish to incorporate.
- Review the subtleties of your exchange and tap the "forward" bolt in the upper right corner of the screen.

Android (For the CoinBase portable application)

- Tap the menu symbol close to the upper left of the screen to open the Navbar
- Select the wallet you wish to send from, situated in the Navbar.
- Tap the "+" symbol close to the lower right hand of the screen
- Select "send."
- Enter the sum you wish to send.

- Use the up/down bolts to switch between sorts of money.
- Enter the email or wallet address and any notes you wish to incorporate.
- Review the subtleties of your exchange and tap the "forward" bolt in the upper right corner

Or then again in the event that you have been given a QR code

- Tap the QR symbol in the upper right.
- Take an image of the QR code
- Enter the ideal sum and press "proceed."
- Review the subtleties of your exchange and tap the "forward" bolt in the upper right corner of the screen. Since you've become a crypto reorder star, you are prepared to purchase altcoins and prepared to proceed onward to figuring out how to utilize a wallet for care.

4. Using a Crypto Wallet

A crypto wallet isn't exactly similar to the ordinary wallet, which you push into your jeans pocket for putting away your fiat cash. Without getting a lot into the hidden innovation (in light of the fact that those of you who need to comprehend everything about everything can Google it for more data), a wallet is a product program that stores public and private "keys" so that individuals can send and get crypto and screen their equilibrium, which is recorded and scrambled on the blockchain.

At the point when somebody sends you cryptographic money, it's simply a trade of responsibility for cash to your wallet's location. To get this going, the private "key" put away in your wallet should relate to the public location the money is appointed to. In the event that people in general and private keys match, the exchange is finished, and you can give a major moan of alleviation that you didn't unintentionally glue in the URL of a dumb feline video on YouTube that you shipped off a companion an hour sooner. There are a few various types of wallets.

Portable

Wallet applications for your cell phone are helpful to get to and can even be utilized in certain stores however are generally not as refined and can't store as much information like different sorts because of a telephone's restricted stockpiling limit.

On the web

These wallets run on the cloud and are available from any gadget, anyplace. This makes it simple for you to get to your crypto. Lamentably, it additionally makes it simple for anybody hacking the outsider organization dealing with your wallet to take your crypto. Pick your wallet organization carefully in the event that you go this course.

Work area

These wallets are downloaded onto a solitary PC or PC and are just open from that point and no other gadget. This makes it less open, and somehow or another more secure, than an online wallet. In any case, if your gadget is hacked, gets an infection, or unintentionally drops off a bluff into the sea, you could wind up without something other than an unrepairable PC.

Paper

This is a technique for printing your public and private keys onto actual duplicate, which would then be able to be (and ought to be) securely put away. This is protected in light of the fact that it is put away disconnected however can at times be troublesome to get to.

Equipment

Regularly as a thumb-drive-type gadget, an equipment wallet gives an incredible harmony between disconnected wellbeing and simple access. With a speedy addition into a USB port, you can approach, send, and get digital currency.

Whichever structure you pick, it is critical to ensure that you duplicate your resources into a wallet when you are finished exchanging on a trade. On the off chance that your crypto is sitting in a trade and the site gets hacked, your coins are effectively available for the taking, and you'll most likely never get them back.

5. Basic Strategies

It's absolutely impossible we can make somebody with next to zero insight into a specialist crypto financial backer by perusing a couple of pages of text, however we can attempt to point you the correct way with the accompanying essential standards.

To be predictable with the general effortlessness of this guide, we'll give you three:

Purchase Low, Sell High

"Much obliged, Captain Obvious," you may be thinking, however in the event that this were so self-evident, for what reason do such countless individuals lose cash in contributing? It is the key law of contributing, yet to do this successfully, you should be straightforward with yourself about what sort of broker you are, just as what amount of cash, what amount hazard, and how long you can stand to contribute? The less you know your capacities, the less you will realize whose counsel to follow, which can eventually lead you to exchange a counterproductive way.

Examination, Research, Research

Simply doing what every other person is doing is a profoundly powerful method of getting messy seconds. Don't simply find out about market patterns. Become familiar with the organizations behind both new and existing coins. Who is an individual from their administration and specialized groups, and what is their central goal for what's to come? These basic advances can frequently remove a large number of the coins bound to come up short from the beginning.

Keep it Simple

From the start, simply contribute a limited quantity to get the hang of the "how to." Don't get extravagant. Get a portion of the top coins and sit on them. In the event that there is one thing that is steady about the unbelievably conflicting crypto market, genuine development requires years, not days. This way to sit and hold and don't get excessively combative and be a wild crypto pirate except if you realize that you understand what you're doing.

The One Strategy

Since you comprehend the fundamentals of putting resources into digital currency, it's an ideal opportunity to examine procedure. While a few specialists may trust it's beneficial to show many years' worth of contributing and exchanging mastery, we comprehend that this isn't commonsense for the vast majority. What number of us has the opportunity to learn everything about the unpredictable innovation of the blockchain world and how it means the organizations and tokens available? What numbers of us need to focus on turning into a specialist in the complexities of resource exchanging? What number of us can sit throughout the day before the PC watching the ongoing patterns on the lookout?

The appropriate response is, a great many people don't. Therefore, we need to discuss approaches to reasonably contribute, expand, and follow proficient techniques without taking up a great deal of your everyday life or turning into a full-time master dealer yourself.

Before most financial backers move into another market, there's a warm-up period that includes understanding a specific resource class and how it may find a way into your monetary picture. With digital forms of money and blockchain instruments, there are extra layers of intricacy, including the thought of cryptography, diggers, blockchains, tokens, hashing, and verifications. There's an extraordinary level of newness and intricacy related with digital forms of money for the unenlightened. However, the ordinary financial backer is relied upon to bounce onto a trade and begin exchanging, particularly in the event that exchanged nothing as long as they can remember.

Expansion is Key

Hand-picking digital currency ventures is a test. Cryptographic money markets are profoundly unpredictable, and surprisingly the most established are still truly in their outset stage. The choice cycle for token postings changes broadly among trades and is as of now not very much managed. Choosing champs from washouts or attempting to time the market has demonstrated to be amazingly troublesome. An investigation by Bitwise highlighted the worth of expansion on account of the limit changeability in the profits of even the best ten coins.

List Style Investing

In 2007, world-well known financial backer, Warren Buffett, bet 1,000,000 dollars that a record asset would outflank an assortment of multifaceted investments more than ten years. He won that bet and pointed out the viability of deliberately enhanced and sporadically rebalanced portfolios. There are numerous crypto portfolios available, however approaching one curated by a real expert, not a self-announced master on YouTube, is another story. These records are simply open to licensed financial backers (those with a total assets of in any event $1,000,000, barring the worth of one's main living place, or have a pay off at any rate $200,000 every year throughout the previous two years) however what numerous individuals don't know is that they all put their portfolio allotment online for people in general! Just by following the allotment rates of every token, you can take your venture and expand it very much like these selective and expertly oversaw reserves do.

Despite the fact that it will require some investment to do the exploration and choose which list reserve you might want to reflect, just as to figure and buy every token independently, fortunately these portfolios commonly just rebalance about once per month, so you will not need to do this regularly. Thus, the writing is on the wall, a manner by which, even with simply the most essential information, you can put resources into crypto with enhancement, adequacy, and expert ability.

Chapter 5. The Beginner's Guide

Exchanging cryptographic money can make a tremendous benefit. Notwithstanding, it's likewise profoundly hazardous. You can win and lose a lot of cash rapidly. This implies crypto exchanging is energizing, and it tends to be hard to hold significant serenity under hefty tension. There are numerous approaches to bring in cash in the digital currency markets, however not the entirety of the ways are viable and safe. I will investigate some demonstrated methods of putting resources into cryptographic money. Here are the main 10.

1. Trade digital money CFDs

Any item with value vacillations can be exchanged a Contract For Difference. CFD is a T+0 edge exchanging device, which permits you to exchange a bigger situation with a couple of capitals. For instance, you can exchange just 0.1 parcel bitcoin with a little store as an underlying edge.

The benefit of utilizing CFD is you can go long or go short regardless of the market moves; you will have the chances for dangerous gets back from business sectors fluctuating. Additionally, exchanging Bitcoin CFD is more adaptable, and you can exchange 24 hours and seven days.

It's likewise famous to utilize CFDs to support actual portfolios for financial backers, particularly in unstable business sectors.

As an ASIC-directed (AFSL398528) forex agent, Mitra de offers 100+ mainstream worldwide instruments, including forex, products, records, US stocks, and digital currencies. Mitra de offers you the chance to BUY (go long) or Sell (go short) on all Bitcoin exchanges, so you can utilize your favored methodology paying little mind to what direction the money is moving.

Pros:

- Speculate on crypto cost without possessing the crypto
- No compelling reason to manage crypto trades or open a crypto stockpiling wallet
- Low store, Higher influence
- The capacity to open long/short positions
- T+0 exchanging is more adaptable

Cons:

- The principle hazard related with CFD exchanging implies influence.
- Not reasonable for standing firm on a foothold in long haul

Presently, Mitrade gives advancements to new clients; You can apply for a 50USD free Trail Bonus to exchange any monetary resources with no dangers, which is useful for novices and amateurs.

2. Day Trading

Assume you are keen on bringing in cash with digital money in a quicker way. Around there, you can attempt crypto day exchanging, which is an exchanging methodology where financial backers purchase and sell orders on different occasions in a single day.

The high instability of Bitcoin and digital forms of money makes the crypto market like a thrill ride, which is ideal for day exchanging, as during the day, you will have enough good and bad times to get a decent benefit.

Preferably, you'll search for a low-evaluated freedom to purchase in and afterward sell it at a more exorbitant cost. In spite of the fact that this might be a little pay, this can acquire extensive benefits to financial backers the since a long time ago run.

Day exchanging is an expertise, very much like whatever else. On the off chance that you set aside more effort to see how it functions, it very well might be a full-time experience. Obviously, nobody will win in each exchanging, yet the objective of day exchanging is just to win more occasions.

So day exchanging requires financial backers more information and abilities. You can attempt to rehearse with a demo account on Mitrade, which gives a 50000 USD practice account. When you have a lot exchanging experience, you can choose to exchange a genuine record.

Pros:

- Relatively minimal effort
- Trading bitcoin on value changes

Cons:

- Need more abilities
- Much time and energy

3. Bitcoin Mining

Mining digital forms of money is not quite the same as the over two different ways of exchanging. Mining might be more troublesome than different ways, yet it very well might be more productive when you mine effectively. Albeit the mining cycle should be possible from a PC, you actually need essential programming, explicit equipment, crypto wallets, and much power. For the vast majority, mining is an exceptionally specific industry that isn't reasonable for singular financial backers. Most Bitcoin mining is done in an enormous distribution center with modest power.

In some cases, the equipment is additionally costly. For instance, during the positively trending market in 2017, the cost of GPU raised steeply, while as the market breakdowns, you can purchase great mining hardware with less expense.

In the early years, bitcoin excavators could acquire coins moderately rapidly. However, by 2019, cryptographic money mining is more convoluted. Numerous expert diggers have fabricated enormous exhibits to mine, making it harder for more modest excavators. Obviously, you can join a bitcoin mining pool to be more successful, however that accompanies a charge. I likewise discover some crypto excavator application in the crypto business professing to help you mine crypto coins. It's more similar to diversion mining. Try not to depend on the application to bring in extraordinary cash for you.

Pros:

- Earning possibilities is higher

Cons:

- High cost to begin
- relatively troublesome

4. Long Term Investing

This is the simplest method to bring in cash with digital currency. Numerous individuals choose not to exchange cryptographic forms of money but rather purchase a specific number of coins and afterward put them in their wallets until the value ascends to make benefits. The reason of long haul contributing is that you have investigated and accept the digital currencies you put resources into will get more piece of the pie after some time.

In spite of the fact that there are a wide range of advanced coins, we suggest that you pick safe and profoundly fluid monetary forms, like BTC, LTC, and XRP. These coins have been famous available. In the event that you put resources into another crypto coin, it very well might be modest, however the coin is probably going to vanish after the market preliminary. Presently, numerous individuals acquire a major benefit from Bitcoin on the grounds that they purchased Bitcoin in the year 2011 or 2012, and they hold these computerized coins for quite a while regardless of whether the cost of bitcoin had ascended to 18,000 USD.

Pros:

- Easy to begin
- Beginner-accommodating

Cons:

- Take quite a while

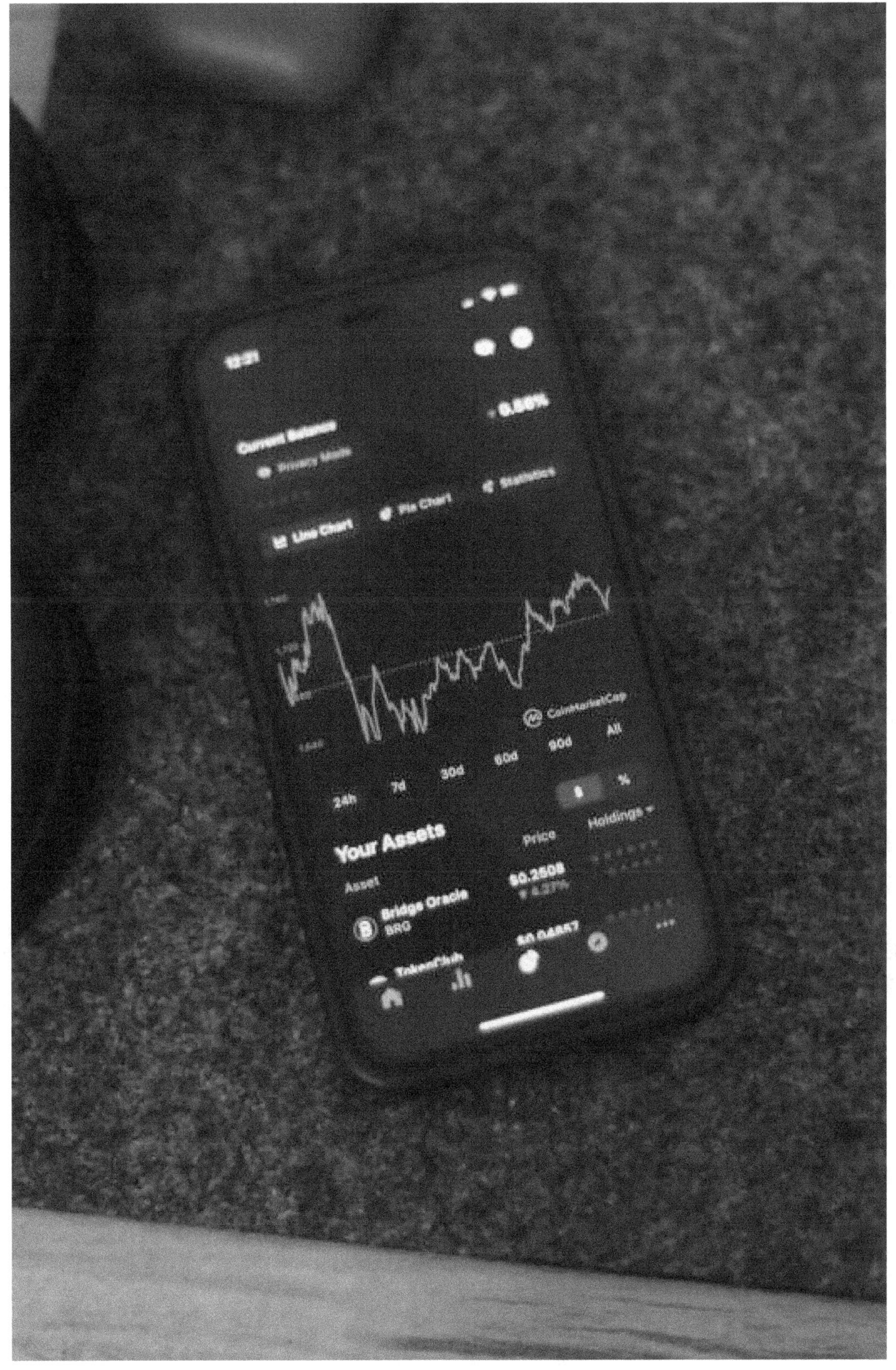
Current Balance
Line Chart
Pie Chart
Statistics
CoinMarketCap
24h
7d
30d
60d
90d
All
Your Assets
Price
Holdings
Asset
Bridge Oracle
BRG
$0.2508

5. Arbitrage

A few financial backers additionally utilize the method of exchange to bring in cash with digital forms of money. This implies when you purchase a computerized coin in crypto trade and afterward sell it on another crypto trade. Yet, truly, crypto exchange is uncommon that likely will not cause you to get rich rapidly.

Pros:

- Instant benefit
- Low prerequisites for section

Cons:

- Good openings are uncommon
- High hazard of losing benefits because of the great unpredictability in the digital currency markets

6. Cryptocurrency spigot

In the event that you are tracking down a compelling method to benefit from modest quantities of digital forms of money, at that point a Crypto fixture might be one decision. A Crypto spigot resembles a trickling fixture. It is a site delivering very limited quantities of digital currencies, like Bitcoin, like clockwork. You need to do a few assignments as per the site necessities.

The crypto spigot site will bring in cash with publicizing and traffic. At the point when you're looking out for the page, there will be promotion arrangements.

Pros:

- Easy to utilize
- Easy to procure coins

Cons:

- Quite a limited quantity of coins
- Need to invest a lot of energy
- It can't cause you to get rich

7. ICO

ICO implies Initial Coin Offerings, which are like crowd funding. ICO permits business visionaries to raise assets by making and selling their virtual money without hazard capital. It can make an enormous profit from your venture, however it likewise brings tremendous instability and dangers. ICO has a ton of traps. You must be cautious about picking the privilege ICO. In the event that the ICO coin isn't entirely significant, you may hazard losing cash. In this way, you would do well to contribute when you think the undertaking is sufficient and just put resources into what misfortunes you can bear.

Pros:

- Opportunity to put resources into point of view ventures at a beginning phase
- Low section limit

Cons:

- Many tricks
- Hacker assaults
- High chances

8. Crypto gaming

This is additionally a genuinely regular approach to acquire Bitcoin, messing around to get BTC; it is like joining the Bitcoin taps above. There will be new titles delivered, and they need to have more individuals download and mess around to make the game better known. These games will grant BTC prizes to clients. Your work is basically to have a telephone, download these games, and afterward sit and play. Subsequent to finishing the game, you will get a specific measure of BTC.

Pros:

- Easy to acquire Bitcoin

Cons:

- Have to invest a lot of energy
- Quite a modest quantity

9. **Be a blockchain engineer.**

Blockchain improvement isn't very different from normal web advancement. Numerous designers have built up their own dispersed applications (DAPP) on certain stages, like Ethureum and NEO. At that point, you can bring in cash by showing advertisements, buys, memberships, and so forth, inside the application. Nonetheless, making and keeping a typical blockchain isn't simple. Above all else, the code is public and apparent to everybody. Anybody can see the code and check for blunders and weaknesses. This permits any software engineer to attack.

Pros:

- High pay
- Safe approach to acquire coins

Cons:

- You should think about coding

10. By advertising crypto with affiliate marketing

In the event that you own a site or blog for crypto, this might be a decent method to acquire an optional pay. The cryptographic money industry, particularly Bitcoin, is developing, however the substance around Bitcoin on the Internet is still "scant." You can accept this open door to make a site work in posting news, tips, and directions for Bitcoin exchanging.

Pros:

- Low speculation costs
- Passive pay
- Flexible working timetable

Cons:

- You should have a site
- You don't control partner promoting programs
- Freelance occupations are not for everybody

DECENTRALIZED • PEER TO PEER

What's preventing fledglings from making a steady pay from exchanging cryptographic money?

- **Make cash with digital currency will take a great deal of time and steady exertion**.

In contrast to proficient financial backers, most fledgling brokers figuring out how to exchange aren't full-time dealers to drench themselves in the business sectors.
That implies they need more an ideal opportunity to get themselves to the level where they can exchange like a star.

- **You have no unmistakable exchanging methodology.**

Ask yourself an inquiry: "What is my exchanging procedure?" If you replied: "System? Indeed, I just purchased and held up in trust, so was that viewed as a system? ". Presently we need to talk. On the off chance that you don't have a reasonable exchanging methodology, regardless of whether it depends on specialized pointers or essential information on crypto resources, or dependent on innovation (algorithmic exchanging), at that point surely there is very There are numerous potential issues that you may experience.

Notwithstanding, first, you need to get yourself and your exchanging style better. Advanced resources are quite possibly the most unpredictable resources nowadays, and yet, fundamental blockchain innovation sets out a freedom to get more extravagant later on.

- **You indiscriminately desire to recuperate.**

The visually impaired any expectation of a bounce back or Bull Run is something each broker has encountered in any event once. That is the reason you will see rehashed updates in speculation archives that, "What occurred in the past isn't a pointer of future value developments." Indeed, there is a contrast between specialized examination and gazing at the screen and reciting "Bitcoin will arrive at 21,000" until that occurs.

- **You are averaging your situation during the downtrend.**

Another difficult you may discover in the bear market is the normal of the downtrend, or all in all, to inundate you on the lookout. Some altcoins are viewed as promising or genuine prospects, however pause and wonder why you continue to stay nearby this coin and can't get out. Purchasing when the market is falling is a decent method to purchase low, however you likewise need to sell when it feels right, or perhaps you should see the cash's decrease significantly more profound before it shows any benefit.

You likely realize that a few group can purchase A for 100, the value tumbles to 80 and still doesn't cut misfortunes as recently suspected, and afterward to 60 individuals who trust that the market will return, go through cash, purchase in to trust you're not kidding "normal" position and diminish misfortunes. At that point it goes down once more, and you become terrified.

- **You totally disregarded danger the board.**

Without addressing why an altcoin (or even Bitcoin) is so unpredictable will lead us to the following justification responding to the inquiry, "for what reason are you losing cash in the bear market?" If you don't focus on hazard the board, you are putting yourself at a misfortune. Ask yourself your present normal danger level by resources and trades? Will I get an opportunity to recuperate on the off chance that one of the coins is delisted or the trade is hacked? In the event that you don't have clear responses to these inquiries - you might be strolling in a minefield.

- **You don't gain from your own mix-ups.**

The last explanation is presumably the most significant. Nearly everybody has begun a couple of times at the screen and asked for an expansion in venture. Or then again a few groups keep on purchasing a sinking crypto resource that is probably not going to recuperate. Yet, they have taken in a couple of things. In case you're committing an error from this bear market, focus on them. It is the expense of instruction, albeit the misfortune isn't fun; in the event that you don't make the most of that chance and gain from botches, particularly because of unnecessary expectation or restricted information, you will lose more expectation.

How to become a professional crypto trader?

The principal thing we will begin with is a clarification of who is a "proficient cryptographic money dealer" and what is "exchanging": In basic words, exchanging implies trading or selling activities between two market members, where exchanging resources change hands.

Digital currency exchanging is a trade exchange between crypto-to-crypto or digital currencies to-fiat cash. Purchasing digital money like Bitcoin for US dollars is a trade activity, which implies you trade your money for crypto.

Being a merchant is something other than a diversion. It is a genuine energy or calling, which requires a ton of time and no less specialized information just; for this situation, exchanging will bring standard benefit.

A digital money merchant is a client of a cryptographic money stage or trade following up on its drive by exchanging advanced resources (cryptographic forms of money and fiat cash) to benefit from the exchanging interaction itself (purchasing and selling reserves). The motivation behind exchanging is to get cash for proficiently performed tasks (shut with benefit).

Cryptographic money exchanging is getting increasingly mainstream. Consistently an ever increasing number of individuals might want to attempt themselves as dealers. There are numerous fantasies around this calling, and most accept that to turn into a broker, you need higher monetary schooling or have an over-created instinct, over-reason, be an expert from God, and so forth Indeed, this would be a huge reward, yet in no way, shape or form an essential. What's more, today, we will demonstrate it!

Would i be able to see myself as a broker after a few effective exchanges?

The notable principle of "novice's karma" applies here too. You can benefit once or even a few times from opening exchanging positions indiscriminately, at the same time, tragically, it works in an unexpected way. For fruitful and successful digital money exchanging, you need to comprehend a few perspectives:

- Current market circumstance.
- How exchanging instruments work (what sorts of requests are accessible, and so forth);
- Understand how to understand graphs. For instance, you need to realize how to check the ethereum cost in pounds on the off chance that you are keen on exchanging this cash pair.
- Most critically, examine exchanging examples and developments on the outline to fabricate the correct exchanging procedure.

A broker's demonstrable skill lies he would say on the lookout, how he responds in upsetting circumstances, the amount he thinks out his exchanging steps, and "fallback alternatives."
Despite the exchanging system sought after, the primary exchanging objective remaining parts unaltered. To be specific, "Purchase less expensive - sell more costly" - the lone justification any exchanging activity is to benefit.

What information do I have to improve my exchanging abilities?

Market examination is the establishment of a fruitful exchanging methodology and makes a benefit. Not a solitary exchanging system, even Buy&HODL, is effective without seeing how market developments work and the primary exchanging candle designs.

Try not to BE SCARED

You don't need to be an expert to begin exchanging! Indeed, even a novice can bring in cash by purchasing/selling digital currencies with the privilege and insightful advances. Experience characterizes an expert, and experience is the thing that you need to procure. Hence, go through this way of turning out to be from an odd one out to a swan! For our situation, from amateur to proficient ;).

From the very beginning, it is critical to comprehend the kinds of orders gave on the stage utilized and what "pictures on the diagram" mean, how to put orders and what instruments are accessible on the stage. Interestingly, this will be all that anyone could need!

We can draw a similarity with power - to turn on a TV, forced air system, or night light - you don't really have to know how they work in the engine. It's sufficient to figure out how to work them. A similar rationale applies here!

MONETARY METALS
TROY OZ 999 FINE COPPER MMB

Is there a simple success exchanging strategy to bring in cash on cryptographic forms of money?

Slight an interesting inquiry in light of the fact that the appropriate response is both "yes" and "no" all the while.
The truth of the matter is that the cryptographic money market is unstable; hence, it generally gives a chance to bring in cash for the individuals who follow the market "at the current second" and ability to utilize exchanging devices effectively.
"Purchase less expensive sell more costly" that is the proverb of any exchanging methodology.

The Buy&HODL system can be viewed as winning under specific conditions. Its substance is to purchase a resource and stand by till it develops. The primary concern isn't to miss the second and sell on schedule. Subsequently, when purchasing a specific exchanging resource for hold it, you need to make a primer investigation and get a few signs that the resources cost being referred to will probably flood. Something else, there is a danger of misfortunes.

How to pick a stage for crypto exchanging on the off chance that I am a novice?

Check the state's public assessment and notoriety. Security is critical! The stage should agree with the most elevated security norms to ensure your information and assets. Discover the rundown of the upheld nations: not all administrations cover clients' entrance all throughout the planet. Check if occupants of your nation can be the stage's clients. It is additionally critical to have client assistance nonstop. You need to ensure you can find support from the client care whenever you need it.

Benefits of the cryptographic money market:

Market instability no monetary market can contrast with the changes in digital money rates. Today, it is the most adaptable approach to bring in cash on exchanging; the cost of certain resources can make x100 in a real sense in a day. Despite the fact that note, they can likewise drop as quickly as they develop.

Cryptographic money accessibility advanced monetary forms are accessible whenever. The digital currency market works day in and day out, and you can exchange, store, or your crypto resources when you need. Namelessness regardless of whether the exchange can be followed - you'll see the wallet address, not the ID information of the proprietor. Unwavering quality cryptographic forms of money are protected. Be that as it may! Just on the off chance that you utilize a demonstrated and secure assistance. Slender discharge is useful for cryptographic money tokens. The less coins were given, the more interest for them.

Cryptographic money is decentralized cash; no single element or middle person controls the exchanges. Low exchange expenses the commission for moving assets is a lot of lower than the bank moves, for instance.

Why stopping? Go, pick the stage, make a record, and begin exchanging. Simply remember one principle consistently do your exploration first!

Bookkeeping and QuickBooks Made Easy

A Comprehensive Guide of 87 Useful Tricks to Hack QuickBooks and Organize Bookkeeping as a Silicon Valley Company

By

Amir Lime

Table of Contents

Introduction

This book is your basic guide to bookkeeping and QuickBooks. If you are a bookkeeper and want to upgrade your skillset and learn more about the QuickBooks software, this book is just for you. You will find a comprehensive detail of all the considerations, the advantages, and the ways you can become a QuickBooks bookkeeper. If you are a beginner and managing finances interests you, you can equally benefit from this book.

In the following chapters, you will find a detailed explanation of bookkeeping and why proper bookkeeping is necessary to keep businesses afloat. With people starting their businesses by the minute, the need for accurate bookkeeping is ever in demand. Small business owners invest in good financial handling software and outsourcing their account management to bookkeepers as affording an accountant is sometimes not possible for a small business owner.

You might question that bookkeeping is not as lucrative but do not pay head to that. Yes, conventional bookkeeping is becoming outdated, but still, there is demand. Most small business owners in the US use the software QuickBooks for their financial recording. Though some business owners know how to use it and keep updated, most of them will require help with crunching numbers and outsource professional bookkeepers to do the job.

QuickBooks was launched in the year 2003 by the company Intuit. After its launch, the company has launched various versions of the software to cater to different business owners' requirements. QuickBooks usage dominates the small business market by 80%. The company provides desktop-based and cloud-based versions of the software. From 2014 onwards there is a shift in trend. Before 2014, the business owners preferred the desktop model, but after the year 2014, more and more business owners are shifting to the cloud-based versions.

A whole chapter is dedicated to explaining the QuickBooks software. We discuss in detail the entire software. The services it provides and how a small business owner can benefit from it. There is a step-by-step guide to set up and install QuickBooks into your computer or other devices. After installation, guidelines are given to set up your account and add the vendor and customer accounts. A detailed explanation about how to enter employee details and how some versions can also manage automated payroll tasks. Reading about all this will make you understand the software's entire system and objective and realize how easy it is to operate. Technology has made even the most difficult and complicated tasks simpler for us. Now, it is our job to use technology for our benefit.

After you have understood the basic functioning of the software, you might want to invest in one. But this is not as easy as just purchasing one online. There are different packages of software available for different individuals. There are four basic packages available:

- QuickBooks Online
- QuickBooks Self-Employed
- QuickBooks Desktop
- QuickBooks App

Choosing the correct package that suits your requirements is also an important and difficult decision. In this book, we give you an overview of all the available packages and their specific features. All this information will hopefully make your decision easy.

In the US, the small to mid-size business market is denominated by QuickBooks users, and the owners are always on the lookout for professional QuickBooks bookkeepers for the job. You do not have to do it full time; you can manage all the accounts as a side hustle because QuickBooks software makes everything easy. You have to setup your accounting needs in the software, and most of the work is done by the software. However, it is n0t as easy as it sounds. The software is user-friendly, but you still require basic accounting knowledge and correct usage of the program. You might consider becoming a certified QuickBooks bookkeeper.

In this book, we have also discussed how in 2021, QuickBooks bookkeepers who work online make good money. There is a whole chapter in which we discuss working part-time as a QuickBooks bookkeeper is becoming a high-paying job. The average income of a QuickBooks professional in the US is discussed along with the US's best cities where you can practice QuickBooks bookkeeping. The considerations you should keep in mind while moving base to become a bookkeeper. California is the best place to be because the money QuickBooks bookkeepers are making there is approximately $10000 more than the US average per year.

There is an entire chapter dedicated to the ways you can become a certified QuickBooks bookkeeper. Sometimes a person knows what he/she wants but is unable to do anything because of the lack of guidance. This book gives you just that, proper step-by-step guidance on how to qualify yourself to become a QuickBooks bookkeeper. It does take time and effort, but you have numerous possibilities and options once you are qualified. To become a bookkeeper, you will need a certification. There are commonly three types of certifications you can choose from:

- QuickBooks Online Certification: Basic
- QuickBooks Desktop Certification: Basic
- QuickBooks Desktop Certification: Advance

The certifications are not just a one-time feat. You must keep your certifications up to date. You will require recertification each year by taking the certification exam. These tests are expensive but worth it.

Finally, we discuss the tricks and hacks you can use to use QuickBooks efficiently and effectively. These trips and hacks make your work easier and quicker. You will have to put in fewer hours. It is always wise to use trips and hacks and make the most benefit of the latest technologies. Sometimes doing online courses and certifications enable you to learn these tricks and hacks. Therefore, it is always recommended to keep your knowledge latest and keep improving your skills. The process of learning never stops. You keep learning throughout life. In present times learning has become a necessity rather than a luxury. In the ever-changing world, you will be left behind if you do not keep your skillset updated.

We hope you are going to find this book informative and helpful for your future professional endeavors. If bookkeeping is your calling, you should pursue it. It is one of the most in-demand services in the small business and mid-size business sector.

Chapter 1. Bookkeeping

In this chapter, we will focus on the basics. We will discuss the concept of bookkeeping and how it is the one-stop solution to all your accounting needs. Before anything else, we will try to understand what bookkeeping is and its importance.

Bookkeeping is an essential part of financial management. Small business owners sometimes try to manage the bookkeeping themselves, which becomes a reason for their businesses to fail. People do not realize that bookkeeping is a full-time job. You cannot manage a business and run numbers simultaneously. For this purpose, it is always wise to hire professionals for your accounting and bookkeeping.

1.1. What is Bookkeeping?

You must have heard about the term accounting. Bookkeeping is just that; it is related to managing the accounts. This term is used for business. The management of the complete finances of a business is termed bookkeeping.

To be more specific, we say that bookkeeping involves recording all the financing situations of a business. Bookkeeping is about keeping a record of all financial transactions daily, the influx and efflux of cash, the Payroll, profits, loss, investments, return on investments, and all the decisions related to the business's finance aspect. Bookkeeping helps the business owners keep track of all the information regarding the financial transactions.

After learning about what bookkeeping is, one wonders how a business owner can do all that by themselves? Not all business owners are literate about managing their finances. So, how can a business owner manage their accounts and finances? The simple answer to this question is a bookkeeper.

1.2. Who is A bookkeeper?

Bookkeepers are professionals who are responsible for managing all the finances of a company. They keep the owners aware of their present financial situation, record all related financial data and the total transactions made.

Correct bookkeeping is important for the business owners as well as prospected investors as well. Bookkeeping information is beneficial for the government and financial institutions as well. It will give a clear overview of the economic impacts of that certain business. Big companies and individual investors tend to research before they invest their money somewhere. The best and most reliable source of this information can be found in the company books. Looking at the books, the investor will decide whether he/she wants to invest in a certain company or project. In this way, bookkeeping is important for the owners because it is like his business introduction to the investment world. The better and more accurate the bookkeeping, the more chances of investment.

(A typical Bookkeeper)

1.3. Importance of Bookkeeping

When people start a new business, they tend to neglect the importance of good bookkeeping. Finance must be taken charge from day one and cannot be neglected for a single day. Now, what does bookkeeping do? It gives the company a tangible indicator of its performance and current situation. With this information's help, it becomes easier for the owner to make proper decisions financially, revenue generated, the profits, the loss, the income goals, etc. Each transaction must be recorded; the cash influx, efflux, credits, assets, liabilities all need to be recorded.

Bookkeeping is essential to keep the business afloat. Bigger companies usually hire accountants for the financial department, but it is not always possible for small business owners. So, small business owners mostly rely on hiring a bookkeeper. There whole accounting companies from where you can outsource a bookkeeper. It is cheaper than employing a full-time accountant, and a bookkeeper can easily manage a small business account. Anyone who starts a new business should never ignore the importance of keeping a record of every dime they spent and earn. Everything should be recorded.

1.4. Type of Accounting Method

Each business model follows one of the two accounting methods.

- Cash Basis of Accounting
- Accrual Basis of Accounting

To implement the bookkeeping function properly, the business owner should decide which accounting method they will follow. There are two basic models for accounting which are mentioned above. Now, what is the difference between these two? We will try to explain:

Cash Basis of Accounting:

In this type of accounting, a transaction is only recorded when a payment or cash is received or spent.

For example, if you buy fifty units of a product and the payment will be done after two weeks. No transaction will be recorded. It will only be recorded after two weeks when the payment is made.

This type of accounting model is now considered outdated in present times.

Accrual Basis of Accounting:

In accrual accounting, the expenses and revenue are put down when the transaction is made rather than when the payment is made.

We use the same example of buying 50 units of a product and payment must be made after two weeks. The record will be entered as soon as the receipt is received and will be recorded as payables. This is the more modern model for accounting and is widely accepted.

1.5. What do the bookkeepers do?

Now that you have a basic idea of who a bookkeeper is let us move to the set of responsibilities and jobs the Bookkeeper carries out. Listed are the tasks carried out by bookkeepers that make it convenient for the business owner to systematically run the business and provide a clear picture of its financial position. The responsibilities of bookkeepers include:

- Recording transactions every day.
- Sending invoices to clients.
- Keep track of payments.
- Prepare and maintain the payable ledger.
- Manage the cash flow.
- Compile and maintain all accounts.

1.5.1. Record the Transactions Each Day

One of the jobs of the Bookkeeper is to enter the transactions each day. These include bank transactions. Nowadays, most companies use software to manage accounts. Some software has a function to generate automated bank feeds, which makes the task easier. You must keep a check on the cash, and precious data entry time is saved.

1.5.2. Sending Invoices to Clients

Another responsibility of the Bookkeeper is to make receipts and invoices on purchases and send them to the clients.

1.5.3. Keep Track of Payments

Once the invoice is sent out, keeping a record of the payments received is also the Bookkeeper's responsibility. To keep a follow-up to receive pending payments is also the responsibility of the Bookkeeper. This is also known as being responsible for the receivable ledger.

1.5.4. Being Responsible for the Payable Ledger

Up to a certain amount determined by the business owner, the Bookkeeper makes the payments made on the owner's behalf. The Bookkeeper keeps records of all the payments made by the business. These include the payments to the suppliers, the extra cash available, and the other business expenses. The Bookkeeper records all this information and checks it every day.

1.5.5. Responsible for Managing the Cash Flow

One of the most important business rules is that a certain amount of cash is always available. The responsibility of the Bookkeeper is to always maintain the balance. This can be done by keeping a record of the day-to-day expenses and revenues. There should always be cash available for the day-to-day expenses. If the Bookkeeper suspects that the balance might be disrupted, he/she can offer advice to the owner by telling them ways to control the outflow and increase the inflow. These devices are almost always short-term fixes.

1.5.6. Compile All Accounts

The most important job of the Bookkeeper is to maintain the account books. The account records should all be up to date. These include all the ledgers. This is necessary for further investments and business decisions. The owner or prospect investor looks at these accounts and makes decisions according to the financial situations mentioned in the books.

1.6. How can a Bookkeeper be Beneficial for Business?

When you have a smaller business setup, it makes sense to manage your account yourself. But when the business expands, it is always a good idea to hire someone to take care of the bookkeeping. In this way, you can concentrate on expanding the business, and your Bookkeeper can take care of your day-to-day expenses. Many people do not hire a bookkeeper to save money but lose a lot of precious time in managing their account that they could be using to innovate and expand their business. Bookkeeping is a time-consuming job, and it should be left to the ones who are professionally trained to do so. They might as well do the job better and take less time. Following are listed a few benefits of hiring a bookkeeper:

1.6.1. Let you Focus on Your Business Strategy

As explained earlier, bookkeeping is a time-consuming task and demands attention to detail. Hiring a bookkeeper will save you all that time, and you will have plenty of time to focus on your business.

1.6.2. The Accounting Cost can be Saved.

If you have a small business, it is a better idea to hire a bookkeeper. If you hire an accountant, it will cost you more money and will become a liability. All the recording and accounts can be easily managed by a bookkeeper as well, and it will cost you a lot less money.

1.6.3. Double Check Your Cashflow

As a business owner, it is wise to always keep your eyes on the cashflow. But sometimes, you can get caught up, and in that situation, your Bookkeeper is there to tell you when you need to manage your cash flow. The Bookkeeper can warn your earlier, and you will still have time to manage the situation.

1.6.4. Be Informed of Current Financial Situation:

As the Bookkeeper is working on a day-to-day basis, he/she will be aware of all the business's financial situations. If you require any help and advice in this department, you can advise your Bookkeeper to have the complete information and explain the clear picture to you.

1.6.5. The Financial Data is Organized

In case you get hold of good software like QuickBooks, the Bookkeeper will work on the same software. The data is kept organized and transparent using the software because the margin for mistakes is highly reduced. The accountant can analyze the same data if you wish to get advice regarding business expansion and investment.

All in all, bookkeeping is particularly useful for business owners and investors alike. If you are not a businessperson and are interested in managing accounts for other small businesses, bookkeeping could be a good profession for you. The possibilities are limitless.

Chapter 2. QuickBooks Explained

With a basic knowledge of bookkeeping and what it means for small businesses, we can now discuss bookkeeping solutions. 2021 is all about solutions. Bookkeeping is a difficult task. It can be made easy with the help of accounting software. In this chapter, we are going to discuss software known as QuickBooks.

1.7. 2.1. What is QuickBooks?

If you are a small business owner and you aim to reach the next level, you might want to start keeping track of your finances. Most people control their finances when they start with a business, but it becomes difficult once the business gains pace. If you wish to expand your business, you will have to become more proactive, take hold of your finances, plan your next financial moves, keep an eye on day-to-day transactions, and organize a cash inflow and outflow system. You should set up a payroll. All the administrative work should be organized. Reading all this must have given you a headache. You were thinking about making some money; how are you going to manage all the financial stuff?

It would be best if you were thankful for your stars that you live in the 21st Century and there is software available for everything. In this chapter, we are discussing accounting software that works like magic. The software is known as QuickBooks. QuickBooks is the perfect tool for your financial necessities.

2.1.1. QuickBooks

It is accounting software that has features to organize the financial aspects of small businesses. The functions of QuickBooks include:

- Recording everyday transactions
- Track and record revenue and expense.
- Report generation for planning
- Prepare bills.
- Preparation of Payroll

The software is targeted towards small to medium-sized business setups. The QuickBooks software has features that make it possible for you to manage report generation, sales, cash flow, billing, revenue, taxes, reporting and expenses. The best part about the software is that there are inbuilt templates for reports that you can easily set and customize according to your specifications. It is easy to fill in data to an already prepared template compared to create by yourself. You can take control of your finances. It is a user-friendly software, but it has a learning curve, and you must have some basic accounting knowledge to operate and use this software. To use the software effectively, you must learn and have an in-depth knowledge of the software's essential functions.

2.1.2. The History of QuickBooks

In 1983, two inventors Scott Cook, and Tom Proulx, created the company Intuit. QuickBooks is a product of this company and was first launched in 2003 and targeted to small businesses. Over the years, better and more functional versions of the software have been launched. It remains one of the most widely used financial software for small businesses in the US. Different versions of the software are available in the international markets as well.

1.8. 2.2. QuickBooks Features

QuickBooks is amazing software with multiple features and functions. Here is a list of a few features of the software.

2.2.1. user Friendly

This software is super user-friendly. It is easy to use and navigate. All the financial features needed for a small to medium business are present in this one program. You do not have to record your data in different locations. This single software manages all your data.

2.2.2. Data Migration

This is a wonderful feature. If you want to transfer any data from QuickBooks to the spreadsheet, the transition is smooth. When there is a requirement to present the data on a spreadsheet, you can easily transfer all the software from the software without manually copying it.

2.2.3 Smooth Navigation

To use this software is easy because the navigation is simple. Everything is displayed clearly, and working is smooth. The program interface is clear and simple. However, you will have to learn and get used to the software before you can use it. You need to learn and understand all the financial terms and data entry methods to using this software effectively.

2.2.4. Smooth Transactions

The bank transactions are systematically recorded. Each entry you make is recorded. You can even set up regular transactions like salary payments, commissions, and bills repeated each month or every two weeks. These transactions will be automatically recorded.

2.2.5. Invoices

You can set up the invoices to be generated. The software can even generate invoices from your smartphone or tablet if they are installed with the software. You are not dependent on the computer system or laptop to generate business invoices. This feature is truly per the present requirement where everything can be achieved with a click of a button anytime, anywhere.

2.2.6. Calculate Tax

The feature of tax calculation is included in the software. To do taxes is always a tricky business. With the QuickBooks software, you can easily calculate the taxes quickly, efficiently, and accurately.

2.2.7. Projections

There is an automated feature in the software that will present you with projections. The software can generate all kinds of projections, including profits, expenses, sales etc. Getting the projections makes it easy to make financial decisions.

1.9. 2.3. Set-up QuickBooks

To use QuickBooks, you must have basic accounting knowledge and your own business. To use this software, you must be organized and willing to manage your finances seriously and as a daily feature. Some people install QuickBooks, put in the money, and forget it for months. Some purchase it and never even learn how to use it. QuickBooks does not work in that manner. You must be willing to learn and be consistent. Consistency is the key.

Let us discuss step-by-step guidelines for using QuickBooks.

2.3.1. Start

The first step will be to install the software properly. For installation, you must decide how you are going to use it. When you start the program, you will have two options:

- Network
- Custom Options

You will choose the Custom settings if you use the software on only one computer and use the same computer for installations.

In case more than one computer will use the software, chose the Network setting.

After that, choose the location or folder in your PC where you wish the software to be installed. Add your details, and then set up your company file. After that, click on the QuickBooks icon on the desktop.

2.3.2. setup

As soon as you click on the QuickBooks program, you will see an Easy Setup Wizard to help you set up your company file. By following the simple instructions, you can set up your company file. If you are new to this kind of software, you will be favorable to take help from the wizard. It will make the setup smooth and easy.

2.3.3. Vendor Setup

The next step will be setting up the accounts for your vendors. You will click the Vendor Center in the toolbar placed at the top. Next, select the New Vendor option, and create a vendor account. To add a new transaction, click the New Transaction and fill in the details. You can even bring in details from MS Excel and MS Word.

Add all the vendors similarly if you have more than one.

2.3.4. Setup Employee Accounts

To set up the employee accounts, click the Employee Center. Then click the New Employee button and then add the related information. After the information, you click the button for New Transaction. Add the salary details and any other transaction related to that specific employee. For salary, you must add the date and time for each month. For that, you will click Enter Time and then add the specific time and frequency of salary. Some employers pay per month, and some pay by the week. Put in the information accordingly.

2.3.5. Set Up Customer Account

Like the vendor and employee accounts, add the customer accounts. First, you go to the customer center, then Add Customer and Job. Here you can add it as an income source. Now add the related transaction by clicking New Transaction. Here you will add the information for payments and generation of invoices. There is a link for Excel as well as Word. You can bring the information from Excel and use Word to prepare letters for the customer.

2.3.6. Setup Report Generation

Next, you will go to the Report Center. All the information added by you can be viewed here. You can also customize the kind of report you want to generate. Reports for-profits, payments and expenses can be generated separately.

Add all the employees the same way if you have more than one.

1.10.2.4. Using QuickBooks

After the set up let us try to understand the day-to-day working of the QuickBooks software. What should we expect from the software? How can we manage our finances? What is the essential feature of the software? All these questions will be answered in the following part of this book. Together we will try to understand how the QuickBooks software works.

2.4.1. Chart of Accounts

So, what can you find on the chart of accounts? It will display the company's income, liability, expense accounts, assets, and equity to assign day-to-day transactions. This is what you will find:

- All the financial information about the company. It has the balance sheets, dividend, savings, receivables, and expenses. All this can be seen in the Chart of Accounts as a list.
- All the accounts related to the business, along with the account balances and account numbers. The details of the account holder will also be shared, like the full names and

contact numbers. All these accounts will appear when you click the List Menu in the QuickBooks chart of accounts.

2.4.2. Other Lists

These include the list of vendors you deal with. All your regular customers and customer accounts are listed. All the items you deal with and their inventory is listed.

How this is favorable for the QuickBooks user:

- You can manage everything in one place. You do not have to manage multiple lists and settings. All information is compiled in one place. Either it is the product inventory or the vendor; all can be managed in one place.
- When you have all the information in a single space, you can move back and forth with all the lists, account details and information. You can simultaneously manage all your financial situations together. Everything is easy to navigate and extremely user-friendly.
- Another feature is the easy addition ad deletion of details. It is simple to add new accounts, and it is equally simple to delete

accounts. Anytime you want to change the existing settings, it is easily done.

- Apart from adding ad deleting details, you can also edit details. Correction and updating details are easy in this software.

2.4.3. The Reports

Report templates are already included in the software so that you can customize them according to your needs. Add the details of your vendors, customers, and items. You must add dates and times as well.

Once you start adding details accordingly and you update daily transactions and activities. The reports will be forming themselves. Anytime you feel like having an overview of your business, you can pull out reports with just one click, and the reports will be generated. These reports will help you make important financial and investment decisions.

2.4.4. payroll

QuickBooks makes it easy to manage payrolls. With the software, you add the information, and the program will itself arrange the payroll process. The software can itself manage the accounts of the employees who have tax exemption. You can customize the settings for other incentives and deductions. If you turn on the setting, the software automatically sends emails, deposits, and receipts.

More than one person can manage the payrolls in this software, the one who has purchased the software has to allow the other users on the network by assigning permission.

1.11.2.5. QuickBooks Versions

QuickBooks is available in different types and versions. Each has a different package and fee. The versions are discussed in detail in the following chapters. Here we will list down the various versions of QuickBooks software:

- QuickBooks Online
- QuickBooks Self Employed
- QuickBooks App

- QuickBooks Desktop Products
    - QuickBooks Pro
    - QuickBooks for Mac
    - QuickBooks Enterprise
    - QuickBooks Premier

Chapter 3. Choosing the Best Version of QuickBooks

With the knowledge you have gained in the previous chapters, you know that QuickBooks is a financial solutions software. It was launched 25 years ago, and it has been the top choice for financial management since 2003. If you look at the company profits, they will show you an upward trend for the last 11 years straight. In addition to that, QuickBooks is used by 80% of small business owners in the US. This information enough should convince you to invest in the software.

Once you have decided to purchase the QuickBooks software, you are faced with yet another dilemma. Which version is for you? As discussed in the previous chapter, various versions of QuickBooks are available.

The QuickBooks family has a product for everyone. Here is a quick assessment of what you may want to purchase.

- If you are self-employed, run your company alone, and are looking to invest in a cloud-based accounting system, you should invest in QuickBooks for Self-Employed.

- If you own a small business and are interested in a cloud-based accounting system, you should invest in QuickBooks Online.
- If you are a small to medium-sized business owner, you must invest in QuickBooks Desktop.
- If you are already using QuickBooks and wish to update to another version, invest in QuickBooks Apps.

One of the deciding factors in any investment is the price range and affordability. This is the approximate price of the QuickBooks Packages available, making it easy for you to decide which product is best for you and is easy on the pocket.

Version	**Usage**	**Price**
QuickBooks Online	For businesspersons who want flexible financial access. This is suitable for small to mid-size business owners.	$25 up to $150/month
QuickBooks for Desktop	Suitable for small to medium size business owners in any sector	$399.99 with a one-time payment to $1,213 for one year
QuickBooks for Self- Employed	This is suitable for individual property agents, independent vendors, and Uber workers.	$15/ month

QuickBooks Mac	This is for small to mid-size businesspersons who have their business set up on MAC	$399.99 paid once

(Prices of Different Versions of QuickBooks)

1.12.3.1. QuickBooks for Self-Employed

QuickBooks Self Employed is the newest addition to the QuickBooks software versions. This is cloud-based software for financial services. It is specially designed for self-employed business owners and freelance service providers. It is ideal for independent workers like Lyft and Uber drivers. Property agents can also use it.

As this is a cloud-based program, you can access it with any computer or device with the given login.

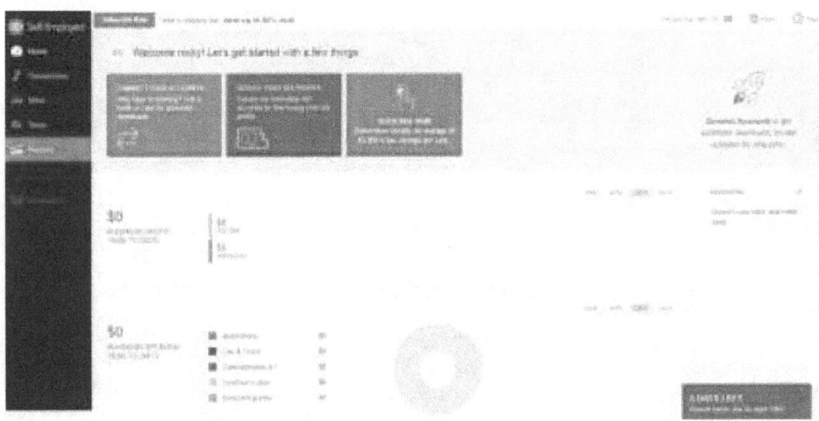

(QuickBooks Self Employed Interface)

(Display of Reports on QuickBooks Self Employed)

Using this program, you can send data to TurboTax and track personal and business expenses from a single bank account. It also calculates the Quarterly Tax and reminds you of payment.

You will find three types of packages available for QuickBooks for Self-Employed:

3.1.1. QuickBooks Self Employed Package

Investing in this package gives you the following features:

- Users can easily connect to their bank account through QuickBooks Self -Employed
- The users can also connect to their credit cards.
- Users can track the expenses and income from the same account but can be separated into personal and business groups.
- The software calculates taxes quarterly.

3.1.2. QuickBooks for Self-Employed Tax Bundle

This offers all the services provided by the simple package with an addition:

- Users can connect to Intuit Turbo Box that enables them to pay taxes online each quarter.

3.1.3. QuickBooks for Self-Employed Live Tax Bundle

Provides all the services as the packages mentioned above with an addition that:

- Users can consult a CPA all year round.
- The users can get the services of a CPA to review taxes.

3.1.4. Benefit

It can track traveling and Mileage. You can enter trips with dates, reasons, and distance traveled. The system will automatically calculate deductions.

3.1.5. Drawback

Does not provide a service to generate invoices and online payments.

1.13.3.2. QuickBooks Online

QuickBooks Online is also a cloud-based financial solutions software. This had become exceedingly popular after 2014 when it was observed that more business owners preferred the online version over the desktop version. After that, the number of subscribers to the QuickBooks online version has been more than 1 million subscribers. This also tells us about the shift of business owners to a cloud-based system and shows their confidence in solely cloud-based software.

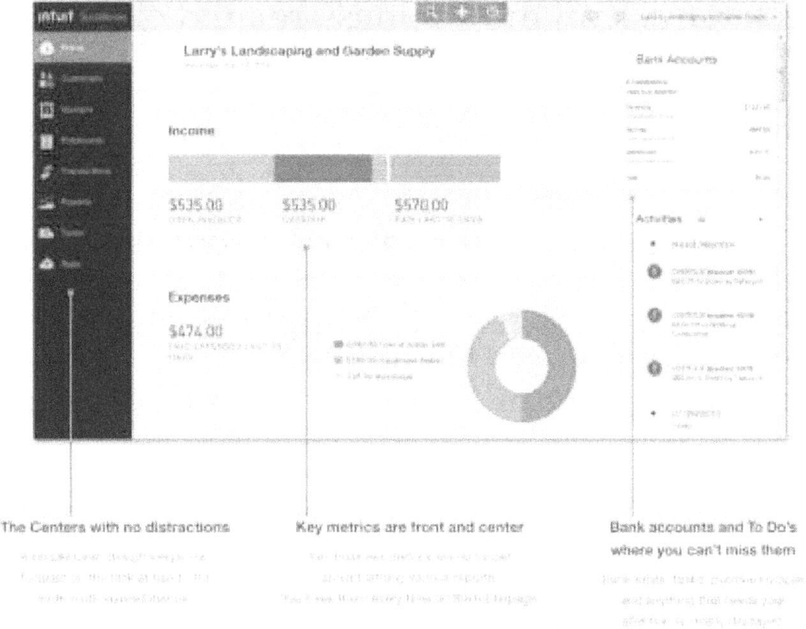

(QuickBooks Online Interface)

3.2.1. Common Features

The common features of QuickBooks Online are:

- Payable and Receivable Accounts:

The program can successfully manage expenses as well as income.

- Invoices and Bills:

It offers recurring or single-time invoices and can pay bills online.

- Management of Expenses:

The software can track all the business-related expenses.

- Reporting:

There are templates of prebuilt reports provided in the software, including the sales and tax reports. Simple Start gives 20 templates, Essentials gives 40 such templates, and gives 60 templates.

The QuickBooks online package does not need to be installed and comes in four packages:

3.2.2. QuickBooks Online Simple Start

The features provided in this package are:

- There is a single-user license.
- You can import your data from the QuickBooks Desktop version or MS Excel.
- You are entitled to consult two accounting professionals (bookkeepers and accountants)

3.2.3. QuickBooks Online Essentials

This version has all the abilities of the above version and, in addition to those capabilities, also has the following capabilities:

- The user is entitled to have 3 user licenses.
- The owner can set up user permissions to determine who is entitled to use the software.

3.2.4. QuickBooks Online Plus

All the capabilities of the Essentials version plus the following added qualities:

- Can set up 5 user licenses.

- The ability to track inventory.
- Users can create and send orders of purchase.

3.2.5. QuickBooks Online Advanced

This includes all the capabilities of the Plus version and the following capabilities:

- Can set up 25 user licenses.
- The ability for automated bill payment.
- The user can set up customized permissions.

3.2.6. Benefits

It is available for iOS, Windows, and Android devices. It can be connected to PayPal and Shopify for transactions.

3.2.7. Drawbacks

All the functions available in the QuickBooks Desktop are not available on QuickBooks Online. This version does not allow the addition of more than one company.

1.14.3.3. QuickBooks Desktop

The QuickBooks Desktop is the most elaborated software version among all three of the versions. Most business owners prefer cloud-based financial services, but if you prefer desktop-oriented software, the QuickBooks Desktop version is for you. This version further has six more variations suitable for different types of small businesses. The six types are briefly explained as follows:

3.3.1. QuickBooks Desktop Pro:

This is good for most small businesses that are not involved in product manufacture.

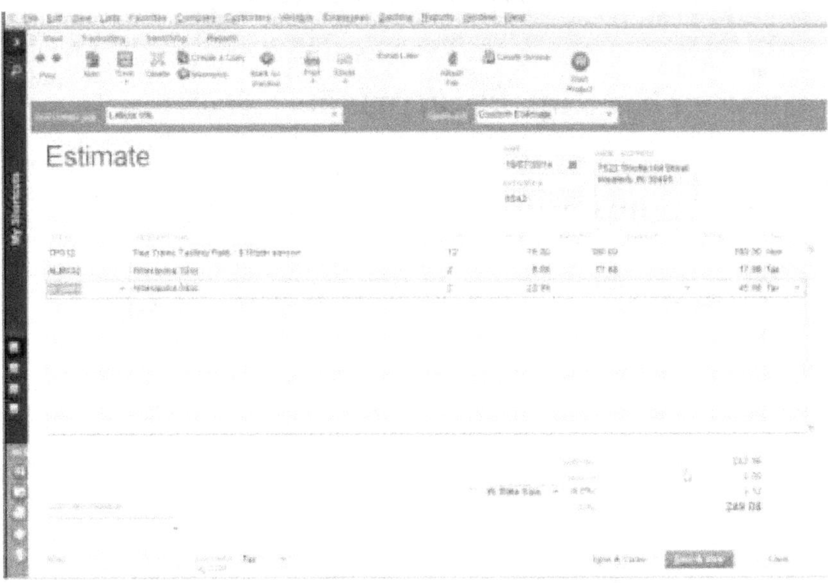

(QuickBooks Desktop Pro)

3.3.2. QuickBooks Desktop Premier:

This version is ideal for businesses involved in manufacturing, retail, and related to charity and non-profit organizations.

(Homepage of QuickBooks Desktop Premier)

3.3.3. QuickBooks Desktop Enterprise:

This is for large companies and enterprises. This version has industry reporting and a custom chart of accounts.

(QuickBooks Desktop Enterprise sales management)

3.3.4. QuickBooks Desktop Plus and QuickBooks Desktop Pro

The QuickBooks Desktop Plus and QuickBooks Desktop pro versions are sold as a yearly subscription rather than a one-time purchase. With these versions, your QuickBooks version is updated yearly, you are entitled to customer support, and your company data will be backed up.

3.3.5. QuickBooks for Mac

This is the only version compatible with Mac. It is like the QuickBooks Desktop Pro version. This is useful for most of the small businesses which are not involved in manufacturing.

1.15.3.4. QuickBooks Apps

QuickBooks Apps are applications that can be used in combination with the QuickBooks software to enhance their features. These are also known as add-on applications. These add-ons can be purchased from the QuickBooks website. Some of the QuickBooks Apps are as follows:

3.4.1. QuickBooks Payments

This can be used as an add-on for the QuickBooks desktop to add some payment functions. This app enables the business to accept payments online as well as through credit cards. This also enables emailing of invoices.

3.4.2. QuickBooks Point of Sale

This is a cloud-based application. It enables the businesses to accept credit cards, track inventory and ring up sales through a point-of-sale dashboard.

3.4.3. QuickBooks Payroll

This app enables businesses to provide salaries to up to 50 employees by cash deposit or check. Two types of versions are available:

- Self-Service Solutions
- Full-Service Solutions

The app can calculate the state, federal, and local taxes automatically.

1.16.3.5. Find the Best Version for You

QuickBooks has been a prominent player in the American market as a financial solution provider. The possibilities are numerous with this software. If you are a new business owner or plan to expand your business, QuickBooks will have a suitable version for you. But how to choose one which best suits your requirements? Here is a list of actions you can take before purchasing QuickBooks software. These activities will clear your dilemma, and the choice can be made easily:

3.5.1. Read Reviews

The best way to get a clear idea about a product is by reading reviews of people who have already used it. See which product is continually rated better. Read about the kind of services the software provides. Sometimes you get more knowledge about a product or service from reading someone's review. Always go through people's reviews and consider the products that most people are buying. Their performance must be the reason for their higher sales.

3.5.2. Take an Online Survey

When you are doing your research online, you may come across some online surveys which ask a few basic questions about your business and earnings. When you have entered your answers, the automated program will suggest the best software for you.

3.5.3. Talk to an Expert.

If you are still confused about which software to buy, try talking to an expert. A professional will be in a better position will suggest you according to your needs.

Chapter 4. The Best Way to Make Money In 2021

The year is all about small businesses and freelance work. In uncertain times everyone is pushing for a side hustle. We often have a misconception that the difficult part is setting up a business; other things follow once that part is covered. We cannot be more wrong in that approach. Though getting an idea, arranging for the finances, resources, place, and the raw material is tough and difficult to obtain, keeping the business afloat once launched is the trickier part. Most businesses come to an end, not because there is a lack of work, but because they could not manage the finances. Not all are indeed good at numbers and finance, and often, help is required.

People have now understood the importance of managing finances and are eager to outsource business financing. Here enters the role of bookkeepers and financial professionals. With the small business boom, there is also a huge demand for financial management. Our focus is on QuickBooks Bookkeeping and how it is the best way to earn money in 2021. In the following chapter, we will see how much a bookkeeper earns in the US. What services you can provide as a QuickBooks Bookkeeper, and which cities are the best for practicing QuickBooks bookkeeping.

1.17.4.1. Salary of Part-Time QuickBooks Bookkeepers

We hear that QuickBooks is a good way to earn money. It is a good side hustle. Be a part-time QuickBooks bookkeeper. No one tells us how much you can make and how much time should be spent to earn a certain amount.

Here we will give you a clear picture of the earnings. A breakdown by weekly, monthly, and yearly earnings.

According to the latest surveys up to 2021, in the United States of America, a QuickBooks bookkeeper's average salary is $50,618 a year. This comes to be around $4,220 per month, around $1000 a week, and about $24 an hour. This sounds very decent for a part-time job. Especially in recent times when we are surrounded by uncertainty, QuickBooks Bookkeeping is a good side hustle.

The figure of $50,618 is the average; it has been reported that you can earn as high as $95,000, and the earnings can even be as low as

$29,000. If you want to look at its percentile wise it will look something like this:

- 90th Percentile earnings $93,500 yearly
- 75th Percentile earnings $ 58,500 yearly
- 25th Percentile earnings $ 36,000 yearly

As the survey is based on all kinds of bookkeepers, from entry-level ones to more professional ones, you see a huge income difference. This also suggests that the more experienced and professional abilities you acquire, the higher you will earn.

The following charts must explain the salaries of part-time QuickBooks bookkeepers in a better way.

- The Yearly Average Income of QuickBooks Bookkeepers

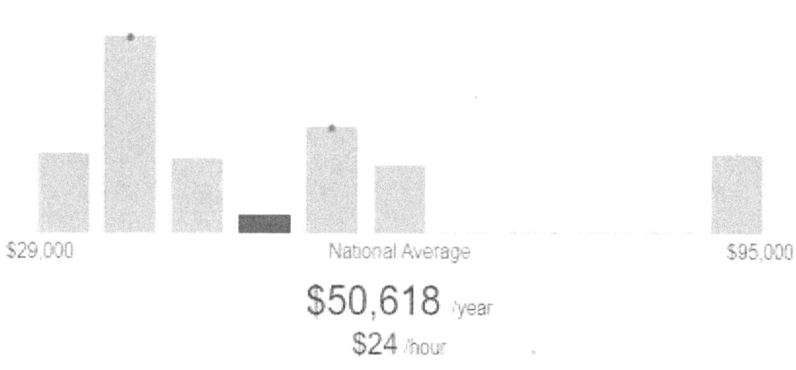

- The Average Monthly Income of QuickBooks Bookkeepers

- The Average Weekly Income of QuickBooks Bookkeepers

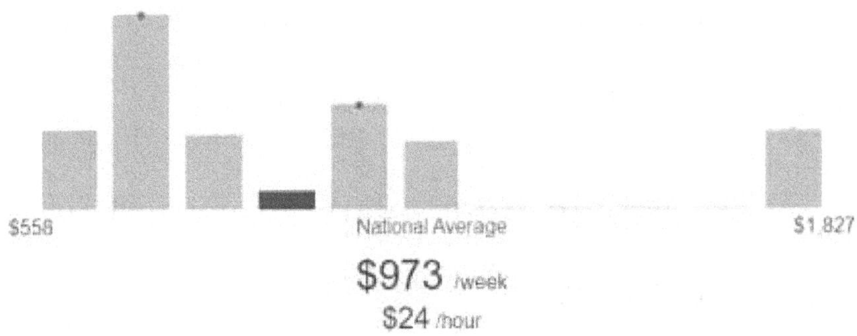

- The Hourly Average Income of QuickBooks Bookkeepers

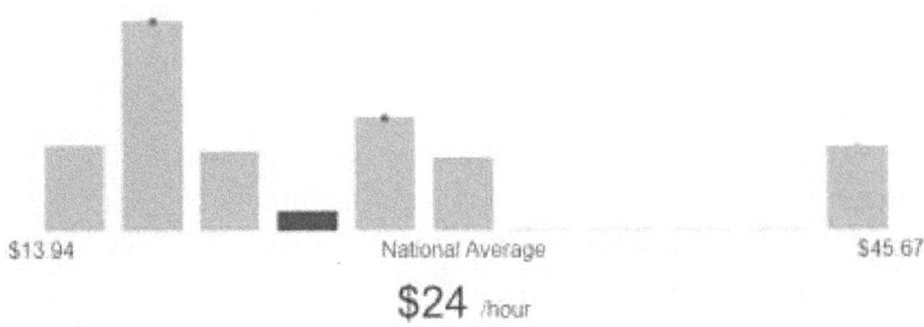

The following table will give you a better understanding of the earning possibilities that come with QuickBooks bookkeeping. These are the results of a recent survey. Thus, they also indicate the present trends as well.

	Annual Salary	Monthly Pay	Weekly Pay	Hourly Wage
Top Earners	$93,500	$7,791	$1,798	$45
75th Percentile	$58,500	$4,875	$1,125	$28
Average	$50,618	$4,218	$973	$24
25th Percentile	$36,000	$3,000	$692	$17

1.18.4.2. The Top 10 Highest Paying Cities for Bookkeepers in the USA

The survey also indicated that the pay varies from location to location. Here we have compiled the top ten cities in the US where QuickBooks Bookkeepers' salaries are higher than the national average.

The state that offers the highest salaries to the QuickBooks Bookkeepers is, without any doubt, California. Companies in California employ the highest paying QuickBooks bookkeepers. The top salaries are recorded from San Francisco, CA. San

Francisco's salaries are around $13,636 higher than the national average. That counts for a whopping 26.9% higher average salary than the average. The second highest is Fremont, CA. The third position is held by San Jose, CA, with a $9,337 higher average salary than the national average of $50,618. Following close behind in Oakland, CA, with an $8,668 higher average. After this is Tanana, AK, with an average yearly salary of $ 59,078, number six is Wasilla, AK, with a higher average of $8459 than the national average. Hayward, CA, has an average income of $58,044 for QuickBooks Bookkeepers. At number eight is Sunnyvale, CA, with an average income higher by $7,268 than the national average. The average salary for this part-time job in Jackson, WY, is $57,870. The last of the tip than in Norwalk, CT.

The table will give you a better understanding of the top ten cities for QuickBooks Bookkeeping.

City	Annual Salary	Monthly Pay	Weekly Pay	Hourly Wage
San Francisco, CA	$64,254	$5,355	$1,236	$30.89
Fremont, CA	$61,596	$5,133	$1,185	$29.61
San Jose, CA	$59,956	$4,996	$1,153	$28.82
Oakland, CA	$59,286	$4,940	$1,140	$28.50
Tanaina, AK	$59,078	$4,923	$1,136	$28.40
Wasilla, AK	$59,077	$4,923	$1,136	$28.40
Hayward, CA	$58,044	$4,837	$1,116	$27.91
Sunnyvale, CA	$57,886	$4,824	$1,113	$27.83
Jackson, WY	$57,870	$4,823	$1,113	$27.82
Norwalk, CT	$57,752	$4,813	$1,111	$27.77

Having mentioned all these cities does not mean that the prospects of getting jobs are higher in these places. This is just an overview of the average income you can earn in these states. Other factors should also be considered when you decide to work in a specific location. For example, you see many six cities from the state of California. You might be tempted to search for work there. But according to research, the job market for QuickBooks Bookkeepers is not active in California. The companies might be paying higher, but the job opportunities are less. It is always smarter to work in a place where the prospects of being employed are better. However, you might be earning more if you locate in one of these locations. It all depends upon the service you provide and the requirements of the employer. It would help if you did your survey before deciding to change your location.

Another important consideration when thinking about making a location change as a QuickBooks bookkeeper is the cost of living. San Francisco may be paying the highest, but the basic cost of living is high. You might be earning more but even spending more on necessities like housing, insurance, and food. This might not prove to be a smart move. For a QuickBooks bookkeeper, an important factor in choosing a location might be the salary and a place with a lower cost of living.

1.19.4.3. Best Paying QuickBooks Bookkeeping Jobs in the USA

This is true for any field of practice that your job prospects and earnings increase if you specialize in a specific field. This part will discuss the five types of specialized QuickBooks Bookkeepers who earn higher than the typical part-time QuickBooks bookkeepers. All the jobs discuss earn around $7,683 to $14,935 more than the national average. This makes the values about 14.5% to 29.5% more than a regular QuickBooks bookkeeper's salary. So, it is highly recommended that you try to specialize in a certain domain to improve your higher earnings chances. The five jobs we will be discussing are:

1. CPA Firm Bookkeeper
2. QuickBooks Remote Bookkeeper
3. Telecommute Bookkeeper
4. At home Bookkeeper
5. QuickBooks Consultant

4.3.1. CPA Firm Bookkeeper

The Bookkeeper associated with a CPA firm earns around $65,553 annually. This translates to a $5,463 paycheck each month, roughly $1,261 a week. In this case, you will be charging approximately $31.52 an hour. If you consider it seriously, this is quite a decent earning.

4.3.2. QuickBooks Remote Bookkeeper

This job fetches you a whopping $64,952 annual earning. This is more than $14,300 than the national average. You will be earning $5,413 per month, which is decent.

4.3.3. Telecommute Bookkeeper

According to the survey, the Telecommute Bookkeeper earns $60 795 per year. This is $10,000 higher than the national average. This brings you a decent paycheck of $5,000 per month and weekly earnings of $1,000 plus. Working as a telecommute bookkeeper, you will be charging approximately $30 by the hour.

4.3.4. At Home Bookkeeper

The best thing about this type of bookkeeping is that you can practice it from the comfort of your house, and you will be earning good money. You will be making savings on the commute time, fuel expenses, and outside food expenses, if you practice work from home. Continuing from home, you will still be earning $8,000 more than the national average. You will be earning around $5,000 per month from the comfort of your home.

4.3.5. QuickBooks Consultant

As a QuickBooks consultant, you can earn $57,986 per year. The good part about this is that you can work part-time and take home a paycheck of around $5,000 each month.

This table will give you a better understanding of the benefits of specializing and the financial prospects related to it.

Job Title	Annual Salary	Monthly Pay	Weekly Pay	Hourly Wage
CPA Firm Bookkeeper	$65,553	$5,463	$1,261	$31.52
Quickbooks Remote	$64,952	$5,413	$1,249	$31.23
Telecommute Bookkeeper	$60,795	$5,066	$1,169	$29.23
Work From Home Bookkeeper	$58,536	$4,878	$1,126	$28.14
Quickbooks Consultant	$57,986	$4,832	$1,115	$27.88

Chapter 5. Becoming a QuickBooks Bookkeeper

Now that you have a thorough understanding of bookkeeping and QuickBooks, it must be clear that in present times the knowledge of QuickBooks is essential if you want to work in the US small business community. Sometimes learning the software is not enough. To get the job, you require to show some qualifications and expertise as well. Unfortunately, we are still living in the workplace where showing your qualifications and certificates is essential to acquire a job. But when we talk about QuickBooks, there is no harm in doing a certification. Doing a certification will open many opportunities for you. No one wants to hire an unqualified person. With this Certification, you will be considered qualified for the job. The Certification might teach you the software's basics, but the actual learning is always done practically. Nevertheless, gaining this Certification is beneficial even if it gives you a head start.

Sometimes you have this clear picture in your mind regarding what you want to do but you have no access to proper guidance. Many people want to work as bookkeepers and want to learn further to upgrade their skill set but there is no one to guide them. The information around us is so much that sometimes we are overwhelmed by the excess of information rather than its lack. Sometimes all we need is a plain simple instruction in the right direction. This chapter does just that. It will push you one step further in the right direction.

In this chapter, we will discuss how you can gain this Certification, how much it cost, how long it takes to become certified, the difficulty level of this Certification, the types of certifications available for QuickBooks; all will be discussed in this chapter. In this chapter, we will discuss:

- The type of investment required for Certification.
- Different courses available
- Information about QuickBooks Certification.
- The course fees.
- The duration of the course

1.20.5.1. The Type of Investment Required for Certification

Getting a certification is a big investment. Not only are you investing your money, but you also invest your time and money in such courses as well. In present times, the world is ever-changing and keeping up with the fast-moving times has become mandatory. Otherwise, you will be left behind. Similarly, if you are a bookkeeper, you must upgrade your skillset. You might be employed right now, but what if the employer changes technology and you are no more required to work for him/her, and they hire a person with better qualifications. For such times it is important to be well prepared and keep up with times. Your aim should be to become an asset to the company rather than a liability.

1.21.5.2. The Different Courses Offered

There are three types of courses offered for QuickBooks Certification. Two of them are for the QuickBooks Desktop, and one is for QuickBooks online. Nowadays, most people prefer a cloud-based financial management system, so it would be wise to take the Certification for the online version. The different types of certifications offered are:

- QuickBooks Online Edition: Basic
- QuickBooks Desktop Edition: Basic
- QuickBooks Desktop Edition: Advanced

1.22.5.3. Information About QuickBooks Certification

If you are working as an employee, getting a QuickBooks certificate will reassure your employer of your abilities with the software and convince them that you are an asset to their company. Certification will enhance your credibility. This will equip you with the expertise to deal with any situation that involves QuickBooks. You will be in a better position as a QuickBooks certified employee to tackle tricky situations involving QuickBooks.

When you pass the exam, you will gain the following skills, and your certificate will be proof of your abilities:

- Easily use the main measures of QuickBooks and manage business accounts on the software.
- You can manage all the accounting functions like Payroll, transactions, invoices, and sales smoothly with QuickBooks software.
- Can solve and manage complex scenarios that come up while using QuickBooks.

One thing you should keep in mind, the certifications are not cheap, they cost high prices. But you should consider investing in this Certification as a step towards your better career. You will get profits from this investment very soon.

1.23.5.4. Why Should You Invest

It is a known fact that QuickBooks Certifications do not come cheap. If you are an employer, you might feel that this is a lot of investment, and the courses are time-consuming. If you have many employees, the cost might be an issue for sure. If you are a freelance bookkeeper, the fee might be a big investment. But consider this a useful investment. This is one of the investments you should make. Some business owners consider it an initial investment, and the profits and dividends are gained when the work is done more efficiently and faster.

A lot of groups are offering QuickBooks certification courses. If you are an employer, you can look for bundle package discounts and monthly packages. If you are a freelance service provider, you should look for packages that offer monthly installments as one-time payments are sometimes difficult to pay at once.

You should always look for online courses. Nowadays, many online courses are available, and you can take them from the comfort of your home or office. This can save you the commute expenses and the time which is wasted with the commute. Always look for certifications with live tutoring. These sessions are more interactive, there are live questions and answers sessions, and you learn more this way.

You should be convinced not to take up a QuickBooks certification. If you are still not convinced, maybe this is not for you. But if you want to further your career in bookkeeping, this Certification is essential.

1.24.5.5. The Certification Fee

Most bookkeepers follow the method that they do their training from a tutor and then take the certification exam. Two groups conduct the Certification:

- Intuit, through their ProAdvisor Program
- NBA (National Bookkeepers Association)

Intuit is the maker of QuickBooks, and they conduct the test for free. However, they cover their cost by making you purchase the mandatory membership, which is hundreds of dollars. You will have to become a member to get access to the test.

NBA conducts the other Certification. This is a much affordable option. If you decide to take the test through them, the fee is $150 for the ones who are taking the test for the first time. This fee includes a practice test and the actual test. At successful completion, you get a certificate. The certification must be updated every year. The fee for each subsequent year is around $75.

1.25.5.6. The Length of Courses

There is no specific length for courses. The courses and workshops are carried out by professionals who specialize in QuickBooks software. The Certification is only a 2-to-4-hour program. If you are already familiar with the software, you might just book your test and pass. But for someone, the learning might take from weeks to months. All this depends upon few factors:

- Do you have basic knowledge about the software?

In this case, if you have basic knowledge and take the test straight away, the chances are that you might not be able to gain Certification. It would be best if you had more than basic knowledge to pass the Certification. You should not take these exams lightly. Since these exams are expensive, you should prepare your best before taking the exam to get greater chances of passing.

- The Certification you might wish to do.

So, there are different certifications offered. In the Desktop version certifications, there is a basic certificate and an advanced certificate. As the name indicates, the advanced certification will be harder and thus require more expertise.

- When you decide to take the test

You must be responsible when you decide the date to take the test. Do not take the test before you are fully prepared. If you decide the test date before proper preparation, the chances are that you might not be able to pass.

Mostly, the tests can be completed in one sitting. The level of the exams is according to the Certification you wish to do. It is recommended to get the basic Certification before you try to obtain an advanced certification.

Chapter 6. Hacks and Tricks for QuickBooks

With every software, you should know about the tricks and tips to make your work more efficient and streamlined. The same is the case with QuickBooks. You can use the experience of others to better your work. You must have heard the term; time is money, and these tips and tricks save your time. And by saving time, they save your money. In present times we are blessed with technology, and we should try to benefit from t as much as possible. The lives we lead in present times are quite stressful, and the work-life balance is frankly off-balance. In such a situation, it is wise to take as much help as possible. That help can be from technology, or you can even benefit from others' experiences and mistakes. Here we will discuss some hacks and tricks the professionals from the field have agreed upon and shared with everyone to benefit from. Here is a list of a few tricks and hacks to make your work quicker and easier.

The trend of 2021 is focused more on cloud-based QuickBooks software. In this chapter, we will discuss the tips and tricks we can apply in QuickBooks Online to gain better results. We have compiled a list of six hacks that you might find helpful:

- Cash receipts should be created.
- Use attachments.
- Use keyboard shortcuts.
- Automate the emails.
- Use QuickBooks Online to track the time.
- Always use the bank rules

1.26.6.1. Cash Receipts Should be Created.

It is always a good idea to organize your working space. The same is the case with finances. If you have your cash receipts created and recorded, you will easily overview all money received at any time. With QuickBooks Online, you can enter the details in the sales center and review the records anytime you want. This is a feature of QuickBooks online, which is easy to use and convenient for financial tracking.

- Usage

How you will create cash receipts is simple, go to the sales transactions and create a file med cash receipts. Next, go to the filter list and go to 'Money Received' and enter the date appropriately.

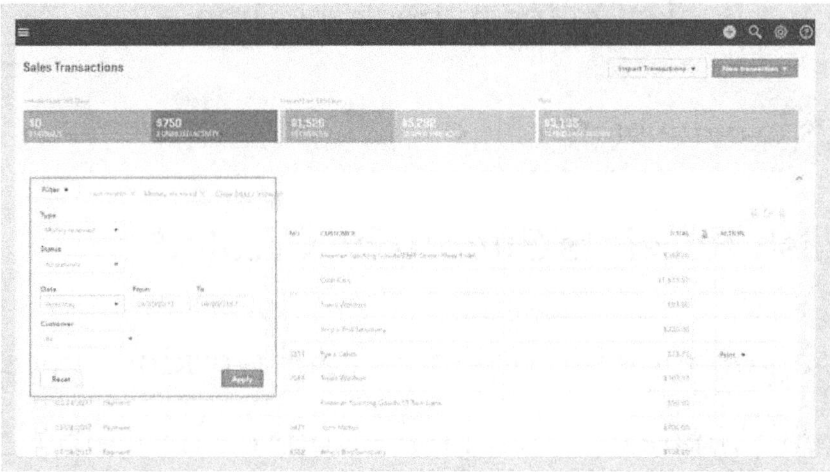

(Cash Receipt Usage)

1.27.6.2. Use Attachments

This is a hack that is overlooked a lot of the time, and most people ignore using it. The hack is to attach all related forms and documents to the vendor accounts to be managed at once. For example, you can attach a W-9 to the vendor's account.

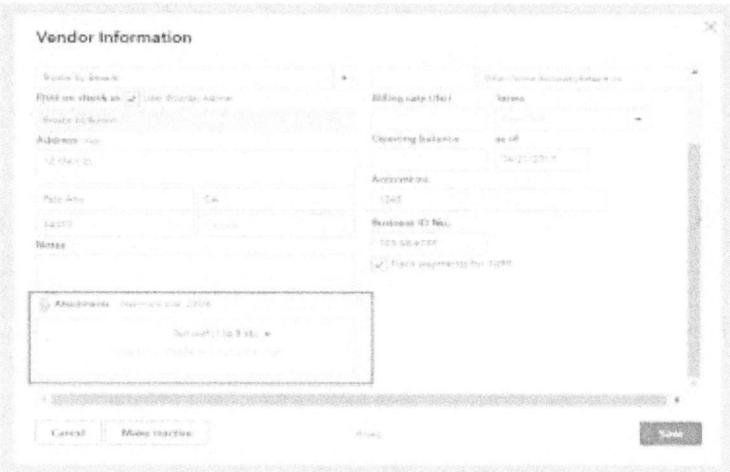

(Using Attachments)

So, when you use attachments, you can also attach the bank accounts' files and the credit card details and statements. When all the documents are attached and compiled in one place, they will be easy to review. Another pro tip will be to use naming conventions. This will make the work more streamlined and easier to track. According to experts, not using attachments wastes time you could be spending on other activities. There is no need to work so hard if you have applications in your software that make your work easier and smoother to operate. If you are using a mobile version of QuickBooks online, you can even take a screenshot of any receipt and attach it to the folder. In the same way, you can even attach the invoices and enter the yearly or monthly estimates. If you have the add-on of QuickBooks Payments, you can even receive payments.

1.28.6.3. Use Keyboard Shortcuts

This is also a huge time saver. When you are working on multiple things, clicking from one program to another makes everything confusing. The same is the case with QuickBooks. When you are managing multiple entities, you need to work fast, and shortcuts are a lifesaver. Following is a summary of all the important shortcuts found within QuickBooks.

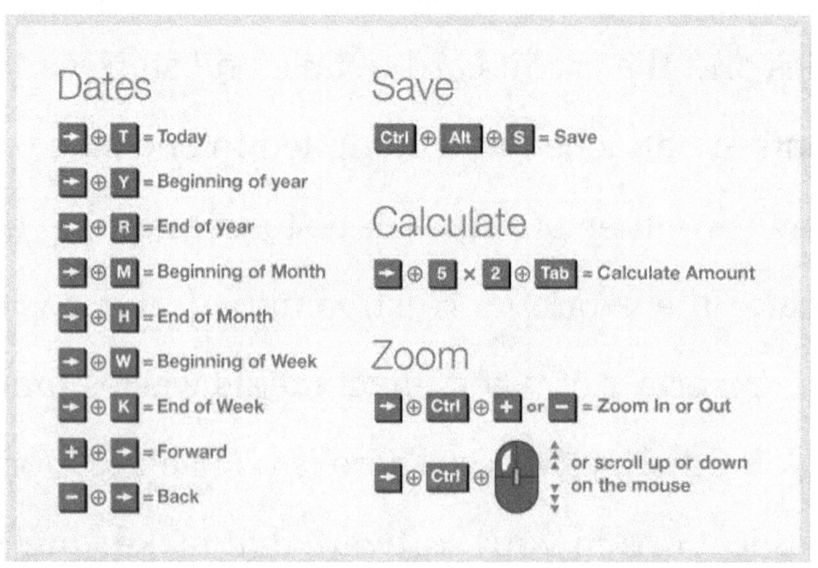

(QuickBooks shortcuts)

1.29.6.4. Automate the emails.

For all the regular payments and receiving, automation is the way to go. You should automate your emails for sales, financial statements, and invoices. You must be thinking about how to go about this? It is easy; you will first set different reports scheduled to email on a specific date. For example, you can set a schedule that emails you your financial statement monthly. You can even get an email for the collection report, and the sales report every week. This will help you keep track of the open invoices.

Apart from this, you can schedule the payments that have to be sent out weekly or monthly. You can arrange for the recurring invoices to be sent automatically by email. Again, if you use the app QuickBooks payments, the received payments can be automatically recorded automatically.

1.30.6.5. Use the QuickBooks Online to Track Time

If time tracking is tough for you, the newer versions of QuickBooks Online will help you. In the older versions of the program, you had to import the T reports to QuickBooks. In the newer versions, you can create the T sheets within QuickBooks online. These are the integrated T sheets. This means that any change, addition, or deletion would apply automatically to the T sheet, and it will be updated by itself. You will not have to manually update the information. This process is carried out in a seamless manner. You can create several employee T sheets and even approve several T sheets simultaneously.

1.31.6.6. Always use the Bank Rules

This is a simple and logical hack. The bank rules are already made, and time tested. If you implement them and set your regular payments to the utilities, vendors, suppliers, etc., on bank rules, the task will become easier. This can save a lot of time for you as well. At the end of the month, all you will need to do is an overview of all the payments carried out in a smooth and streamlined fashion.

These hacks and tips may seem simple but implementing them can save you hours and hours' worth of labor. There will be far fewer things on your mind. It is a one-time setup, and it will be automated from then on. You will easily manage the payments, receiving, employee timesheets, Payroll, and everything else with ease, and you will become less stressed.

Chapter 7. QuickBooks Usage in Small Businesses

Many small businesses use QuickBooks to manage their finances. The software takes care of their bill payments, monitors their cash flow, and manages invoices. QuickBooks is a good software to generated automated monthly financial reports as well as yearly financial reports. Some business owners manage their accounts themselves and are pro users of the software, but most business owners employ professionals to manage their accounts. QuickBooks certified bookkeepers are employed by small to mid-size business owners to manage their accounts.

Small business owners use QuickBooks for several functions and use. Following are the functions for which the small business owners use QuickBooks:

- Make and track invoices.
- Monitor expenses and other bills.
- Generate business and financial statements.
- Manage payroll.
- Do the inventory.

- Simplify taxes.
- Online payments.
- Record Receipts.
- Manage mileage.

1.32.7.1. Make and Track Invoices

The software has the option to create invoices, and you can easily print them or directly send them to your customers. Each invoice generated by the software will be automatically recorded in the system. In this way, you can track all the amount that has already been paid, and the receivables will also be displayed.

1.33.7.2. Monitor Expenses and Other Bills

You have an option to link the QuickBooks software to your accounts and credit cards. This will enable the program to record all payments and bills automatically and keep a record. It will be available for your view whenever you require.

You can enter other bills you receive in the system and take care of the payables. This will help you keep track of your expenses and payables. The software will make sure you do not miss your payments. If you attach the QuickBooks payment app, the payments can even be managed automatically.

1.34.7.3. Generate Business Financial Statements

The software can generate financial statements that will give you an overview of your business performance. The kind of statements you can generate with the QuickBooks software are:

- Cashflow Statement
- Profit and Loss Statement
- Balance Sheets

1.35.7.4. Manage Payroll

The software can manage the Payroll and working hours of each employee automatically. You must create a separate account for each employee, enter each employee's information, and schedule the salary, deductions, schedules, and hours. All can be managed automatically by the software. If you use the software, you can easily manage:

- Payment to the employees can be made by checks or cash.
- The taxes can be deducted automatically, and the tax-exempt employee payments are also managed.
- The software fills tax forms automatically
- The payroll taxes can be managed automatically.

1.36.7.5. Do the Inventory.

The software manages the inventory. It records the quantities and keeps track of the total cost of inventory. The software will indicate when the inventory is getting low, and there is a need to replenish. This all is not done automatically, you will have to enter the amounts manually, but they will be managed and calculated automatically.

1.37.7.6. Simplify Taxes

Taxes is one of the most difficult parts of the business. Most people are fearful of taxes, and in the end, their taxes are piled up. QuickBooks takes care of your taxes. The Tax becomes difficult because your financial statements are not in order. QuickBooks makes the financial statements simplified, and you can easily print them out and let a tax preparer assess the statements and use the required information.

1.38.7.7. Online Payments

The QuickBooks Payments app enables you to accept payments directly from your customers. This app is integrated into the software, so all the payments are recorded in the system automatically.

1.39.7.8. Record Receipts

The QuickBooks app makes it possible for the business owner to upload all the payment and expense receipts to the software, and they can be easily scanned and recorded in the system.

1.40.7.9. Manage Mileage

If you use your vehicle for business purposes, a tax deduction is applied. But to receive the tax deduction, you will have to prove your traveling. You get a deduction of 57.5 cents per mile. To record the miles, you can link QuickBooks Online to your vehicle's GPS, and it will easily record your miles, date, and time

Write a sneak peak on how to earn passive income with crypto

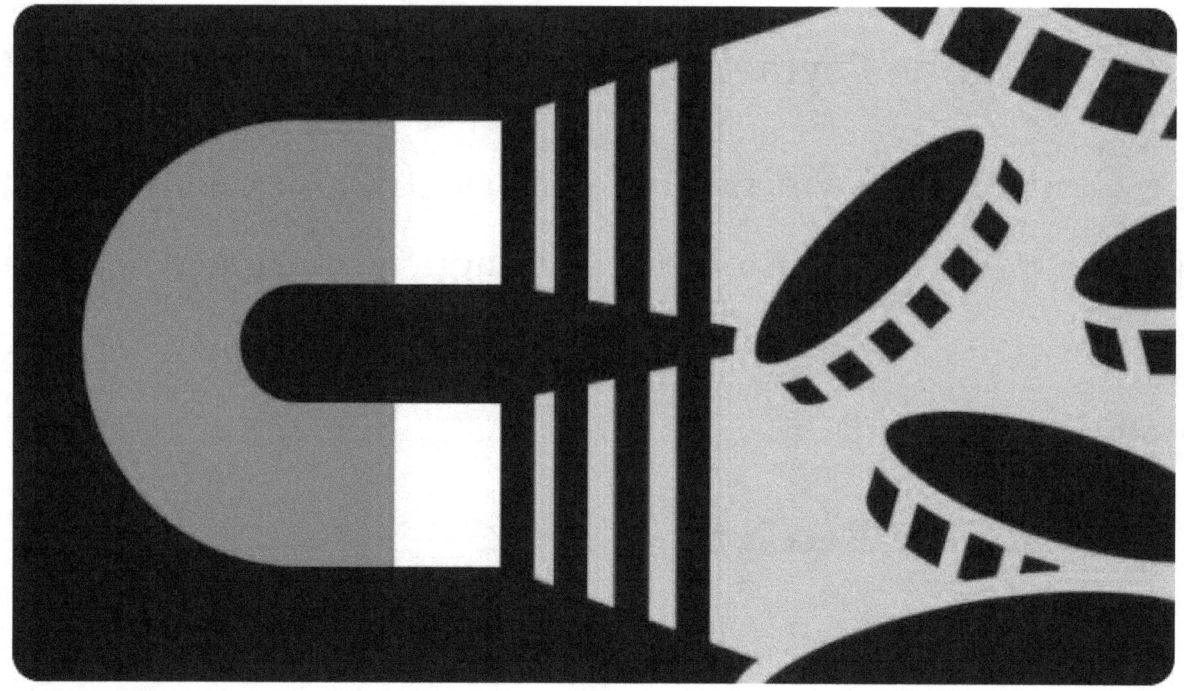

What is passive income?

Trading or making an investment in projects is one way to make cash in the blockchain enterprise. However, that usually calls for designated research and a sizeable investment of time - however it nonetheless receivers guarantee a reliable source of earnings.

Even the great traders can revel in prolonged periods of loss, and one of the methods to continue to exist them is to have alternative resources of income.

There are different techniques than buying and selling or making an investment that allows you to growth your cryptocurrency holdings. These can pay ongoing income just like earning hobby, but most effective require some effort to set up and little or no effort to hold.

This way, you can have several streams of income that could add as much as a sizeable quantity in aggregate with each other.

This article will go through some of the methods that you could earn passive profits with crypto.

What are the ways you can earn passive income with crypto?

Mining:

Mining essentially manner the usage of computing electricity to comfy a community to receive praise. Although it does no longer require you to have cryptocurrency holdings, it's far the oldest method of income passive profits inside the cryptocurrency space.

In the early days of Bitcoin, mining on a regular Central Processing Unit (CPU) was a possible answer. As the community hash fee multiplied, the maximum of the miners shifted to using more powerful Graphics Processing Units (GPUs). As the competition elevated, even greater, it has nearly exclusively turn out to be the playing field of Application-Specific Integrated Circuits (ASICs) - electronics that use mining chips tailor-made for this precise reason.

The ASIC enterprise is very aggressive and dominated by way of groups with extensive sources to be had to install on research and improvement. By the time these chips arrive at the retail marketplace, they may be in all likelihood already outdated and could take a large amount of mining time to interrupt even.

As such, Bitcoin mining has typically turn out to be a corporate enterprise in preference to a feasible supply of passive income for a median character.

On the opposite hand, mining decrease the hash rate Proof of Work coins can still be a profitable undertaking for a few. On those networks, using GPUs can nonetheless be possible. Mining lesser-acknowledged cash deliver a better ability reward however include higher hazard. The mined cash would possibly become nugatory overnight, bring little liquidity, experience a Trojan horse, or see themselves hindered by using many other elements.

It is well worth noting that putting in place and retaining mining gadgets calls for an initial funding and a few technical expertises.

- **How to Mine Bitcoins**

Miners are becoming paid for his or her work as auditors. They are doing the paintings of verifying the legitimacy of Bitcoin transactions. This convention is supposed to maintain Bitcoin user's sincerity and changed into conceived by way of Bitcoin's founder, Satoshi Nakamoto. By verifying transactions, miners are helping to prevent the "double-spending problem."

Double spending is a scenario wherein a Bitcoin owner illicitly spends the equal bitcoin twice. With bodily forex, this isn't an issue: once you hand a person a $20 invoice to shop for a bottle of vodka, you not have it, so there is no threat you could use that identical $20 bill to buy lotto tickets round the corner. While there is the possibility of counterfeit coins being made, it isn't exactly similar to literally spending the identical greenback twice. With digital forex, however, because the Investopedia dictionary explains, "there is a danger that the holder ought to make a replica of the digital token and send it to a service provider or some other birthday celebration at the same time as preserving the authentic."

Let's say you had one valid $20 invoice and one counterfeit of that equal $20. If you were to try to spend each the actual invoice and the fake one, someone that took the trouble of looking at both of the bills' serial numbers would see that they had been the equal quantity, and accordingly one in every one of them needed to be false. What a Bitcoin miner does is similar to that—they test transactions to make certain that users have not illegitimately attempted to spend the same bitcoin two times. This isn't always an ideal analogy—we will explain in more detail beneath.

Once miners have confirmed 1 MB (megabyte) well worth of Bitcoin transactions, referred to as a "block," the ones miners are eligible to be rewarded with an amount of bitcoin (extra about the bitcoin reward below as nicely). The 1 MB restriction became set by means of Satoshi Nakamoto, and is an issue of controversy, as some miners believe the block size needs to be increased to house greater statistics, which might effectively imply that the bitcoin network could process and verify transactions faster.

Note that verifying 1 MB well worth of transactions makes a coin miner eligible to earn bitcoin—not all and sundry who verifies transactions will receive a commission out.

1MB of transactions can theoretically be as small as one transaction (although this isn't always at all common) or numerous thousand. It relies upon how a whole lot of facts the transactions soak up.

"So in the end that paintings of verifying transactions, I would possibly nonetheless no longer get any bitcoin for it?"

That is accurate.

To earn bitcoins, you need to fulfill two conditions. One is an issue of effort; one is a matter of success.

1) You must verify ~1MB really worth of transactions. This is the easy part.

2) You ought to be the primary miner to reach the right solution, or closest solution, to a numeric hassle. This system is likewise known as evidence of work.

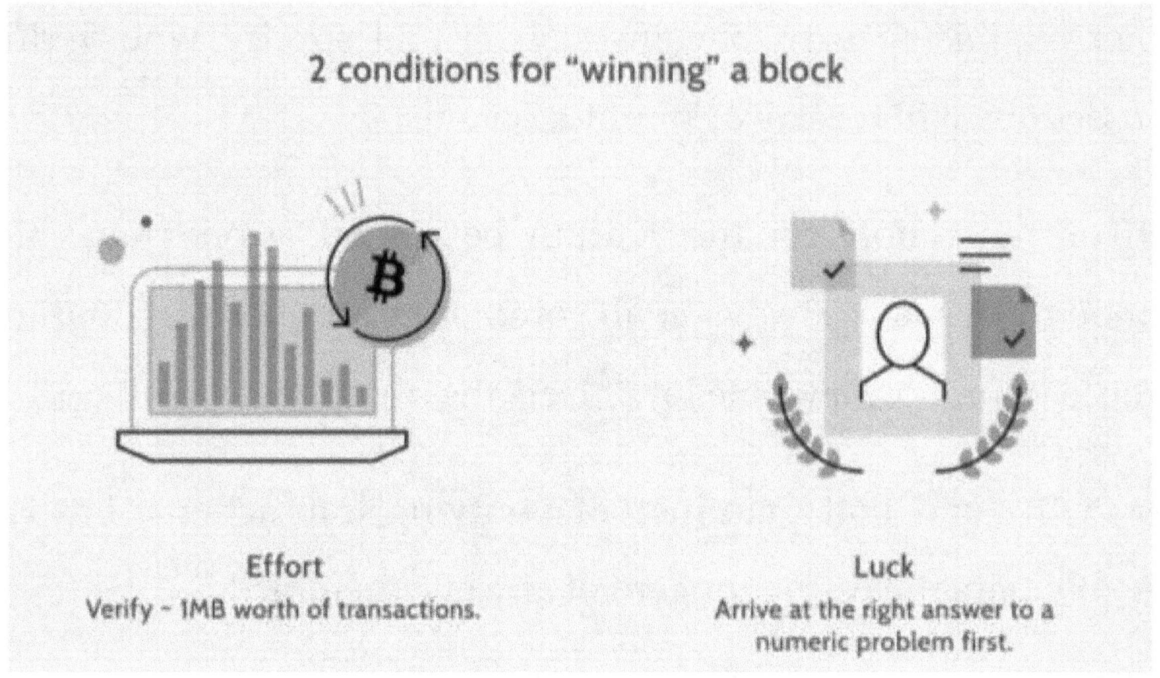

Staking:

Staking is essentially a less resource-in-depth opportunity to mining. It normally involves preserving finances in a suitable pocket and acting various community functions (together with validating transactions) to get hold of staking rewards. The stake (meaning the token conserving) incentivizes the protection of the network's protection through ownership.

Staking networks use Proof of Stake as their consensus set of rules. Other versions of it exist, which include Delegated Proof of Stake or Leased Proof of Stake.

Typically, staking entails setting up a staking wallet and simply maintaining the coins. In a few instances, the procedure includes adding or delegating the price range to a staking pool. Some exchanges will try this for you. All you need to do is hold your tokens at the trade and all the technical requirements could be taken care of.

Staking may be a wonderful manner to grow your cryptocurrency holdings with minimal effort. However, some staking projects hire strategies that artificially inflate the projected staking returns charge. It is essential to research token economics models as they could correctly mitigate promising staking praise projections.

Binance Staking supports an extensive variety of cash with the purpose to earn you staking rewards. Simply deposit the cash on Binance and comply with the manual to get started.

Lending:

Lending is a very passive way to earn interest in your cryptocurrency holdings. There are many peer-to-peer (P2P) lending platforms that permit you to lock up your funds for a time period to later gather interest payments. The interest charge can either be fixed (set through the platform) or set via you primarily based on the cutting-edge market price.

Some exchanges with margin trading have this feature implemented natively on their platform.

This technique is ideal for lengthy-time period holders who need to boom their holdings with little effort required. It is well worth noting that locking funds in a clever contract constantly carries the threat of insects.

Binance Earn offers a selection of alternatives that assist you to earn hobby on your holdings.

Crypto lending for investors

To make it clearer allow's take an example: You are the satisfied proprietor of 10 bitcoins and also you would love to generate a regular passive income along with your bitcoins. By depositing these 10 bitcoins at the pockets of crypto lending platforms, you may receive weekly (or monthly) pastimes from it. For bitcoin lending, these hobby charges typically are from three% to 7% at the same time as they can be loads better (up to 17%) as an example on the more strong property such as stablecoins (e.G. USD Coin, True USD, Binance USD).

And what is even more exciting with those funding types in comparison to others including peer-to-peer lending, ii's that with crypto-backed lending, borrowers should stake their personal cryptocurrency as protection and ensures mortgage repayment. So in case, the borrower makes a decision now not to pay off the loan, the investors can just promote the cryptocurrency belongings to cover the loss.

Naturally, every now and then borrowers don't repay their loans. But due to the fact funding platforms require debtors to stake 25 to 50% of the mortgage in crypto, structures are commonly capable of getting better most of the losses and avoid traders losing cash.

Crypto lending to borrow

So we mentioned all this as an funding, but allows not forget the borrowing side of it!

If you are studying this text, you are maximum probable to believe in the future of crypto. Thus retaining your crypto for the long term is vital.

Cryptocurrency lending permits you to borrow physical money (e.g. USD, EUR, CAD) while you need it in order to avoid having to promote your crypto in case of an emergency.Jef wef

How crypto lending works?

Who is involved?

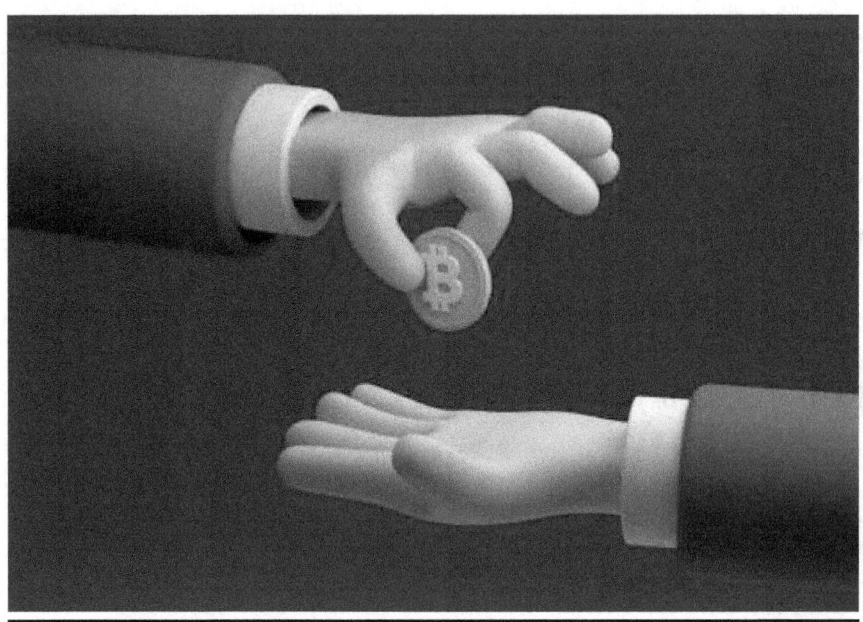

Lenders and borrowers in cryptocurrency lending are linked through a 3rd celebration, in this example, an online crypto lending platform, which acts as a relied-on middleman.

So, for this form of lending to take place, there should be 3 events involved: lenders, debtors, and lending systems:

- The lenders or buyers who want to lend crypto. This will be someone holding cryptocurrencies anticipating the price to soar

(HODL-ers), or just a crypto aficionado seeking to grow his assets' output.

- The crypto lending platform takes care of the transaction related to lending and borrowing. When it involves these systems, we've got decentralized platforms, self-sustaining platforms, and centralized structures with a group of individuals or corporations working at the back of the curtains.

- The borrowers trying to gain price range for something purposes. This may be a person or an enterprise searching out investment and need to use crypto or fiat assets as collateral with a purpose to get funding.

Detailed steps of the process

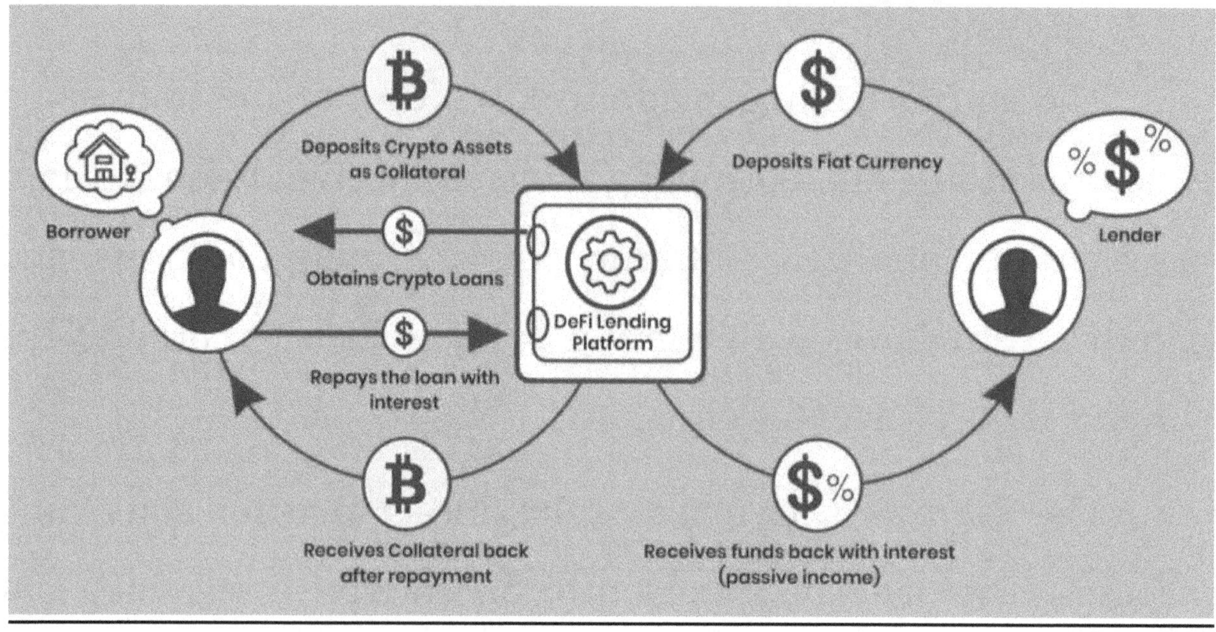

Step 1: The borrower taking place a platform are requests a crypto mortgage (backing it up with his crypto)

Step 2: Once the platform every day the loan request, the borrower stakes his crypto collateral. The borrower won't be able to get lower back the stakes amount till he funds back his entire loan.

Step 3: Investors (lenders) fund the mortgage robotically through the platform. Usually, this technique is invisible for traders for whom the stability of crypto on their accounts could be unchanged.

Step 4: Regularly pursuits are paid to investors (normally on a weekly or month-to-month bases, and infrequently at the give up of the lending duration).

Step 5: Once the borrower paid lower back the loan, he acquired back his crypto collateral.

While cryptocurrency lending is different from platform to platform, the overall idea is the identical for all structures.

In a few cases, cryptocurrency lending also makes use of smart contracts, making the entire procedure of lending and borrowing safer in that the contract itself enforces the terms.

Running a Lightning node:

The Lightning Network is a 2d-layer protocol that runs on top of a blockchain, which includes Bitcoin. It is an off-chain micropayment network, which means that it can be used for instant transactions that aren't right now transferred to the underlying blockchain.

Typical transactions on the Bitcoin network are one-directional, which means that if Alice sends a bitcoin to Bob, Bob cannot use the equal payment channel to send that coin back to Alice. The

Lightning Network, but, uses bidirectional channels that require the 2 individuals to agree on the terms of the transaction ahead.

Lightning nodes provide liquidity and growth the potential of the Lightning Network with the aid of locking up bitcoin into charge channels. They then collect the expenses of the payments running through their channels.

Running a Lightning node may be a project for a non-technical bitcoin holder, and the rewards heavily rely on the overall adoption of the Lightning Network.

Affiliate programs

Some crypto businesses will reward you for purchasing extra customers onto their platform. These include affiliate links, referrals, or a few different bargains provided to new customers who are introduced to the platform by using you.

If you have got a larger social media following, associate packages may be an exceptional way to earn some facet profits. However, to avoid spreading the word on low-pleasant tasks, it is constantly well worth doing some research on the services ahead.

If you are interested by earning passive profits with Binance, be a part of the Binance Affiliate Program and get rewarded while you introduce the arena to Binance!

Masternodes

In simple phrases, a master node is similar to a server however is one which runs in a decentralized community and has functionality that different nodes on the community do no longer.

Token projects have a tendency to provide out unique privileges simplest to actors who have a excessive incentive in retaining community balance. Masternodes usually require a substantial prematurely funding and a considerable amount of technical expertise to set up.

For some masternodes, however, the requirement of token holding may be so excessive that it efficiently makes the stake illiquid. Projects with masternodes additionally tend to inflate the projected go back costs, so it is constantly important to Do Your Own Research (DYOR) before making an investment in a single.

Forks and airdrops

Taking benefit of a difficult fork is a exceptionally truthful tactic for traders. It merely requires preserving the forked cash on the date of the hard fork (commonly decided by block top). If there are two or more competing chains after the fork, the holder will have a token balance on every one.

Airdrops are much like forks, in that they best require ownership of a pockets deal with on the time of the airdrop. Some exchanges will do airdrops for his or her users. Note that receiving an airdrop will never require the sharing of personal keys - a condition that could be a telltale signal of a rip-off.

Blockchain-primarily based content material introduction structures

The creation of dispensed ledger technology has enabled many new kinds of content material platforms. These permit content material creators to monetize their content material in several specific approaches and without the inclusion of intrusive commercials.

In this kind of device, content material creators maintain possession of their creations and normally monetize attention in a few way. This can require plenty of work first of all but can offer a constant source of earnings as soon as a more massive backlog of content material is ready.

What are the risks of earning passive income with crypto?

Buying a low-best asset: Artificially inflated or misleading go-back rates can lure investors into shopping an asset that in any other case holds little or no value. Some staking networks undertake a multi-token system in which the rewards are paid in a 2nd token, which creates steady promote stress for the praise token.

- **User errors:** As the blockchain industry remains in its infancy, putting in place and preserving these assets of earnings calls for the technical know-how and an investigative mindset. For a few holders, it might be best to wait till those services grow to be greater person-pleasant or best use ones that require minimal technical competence.

- **Lockup periods:** Some lending or staking techniques require you to fasten up your finances for a fixed amount of time. This makes your holdings efficiently illiquid for that point, leaving you prone for any occasion which can negatively affect the charge of your asset.

- **Risk of bugs:** Locking up your tokens in a staking pocket or a clever agreement always contains the chance of insects. Usually, there are a couple of choices to be had with numerous degrees of pleasure. It is imperative to analyze these selections before committing to one. Open-supply software might be a very good place to begin, as the one's options are a minimum of audited by way of the network.

Closing thoughts

Some ways to generate passive income in the blockchain enterprise are growing and gaining reputation. Blockchain corporations have additionally been adopting some of those strategies, presenting services commonly referred to as generalized mining.

As the products are becoming extra reliable and relaxed, they might soon become a legitimate alternative for a consistent supply of profits.

Conclusion

If you have read the whole book, many of your doubts must have been cleared regarding bookkeeping and QuickBooks. This is an amazing opportunity for you to avail yourself if you want to take up bookkeeping as a profession. It is always a better idea to keep up with the current trends and technology because it ensures better job and working opportunities. Therefore, we have mentioned QuickBooks. Being a QuickBooks certified bookkeeper gives you an edge in business. This is because most small to mid-size businesses have installed the QuickBooks software for their financial management. There are different versions of QuickBooks available:

- QuickBooks Self-Employed
- QuickBooks Online
- QuickBooks Desktop
- QuickBooks Apps

QuickBooks is user-friendly and is compatible with other programs like MS Word and MS excel. Different versions are available that are compatible with iOS, android, windows, and Mac operating systems.

It will be a good idea to specialize in cloud-based QuickBooks software because, as of 2014, more and more business owners are interested in keeping their records on the cloud-based package offered by QuickBooks. If you are planning to get your Certification any time soon, the cloud-based product should be your focus. There is a basic course offered in QuickBooks Online; you should consider that.

Another consideration when thinking about QuickBooks bookkeeping seriously is what type of Bookkeeper you are going to be. According to a survey, these five types of part-time QuickBooks bookkeepers are making the highest number of average incomes:

- CPA Firm Bookkeeper
- QuickBooks Remote Bookkeeper

- Telecommute Bookkeeper
- At home Bookkeeper
- QuickBooks Consultant

The next most important point to think about is your location. At different locations in America, bookkeepers make different yearly incomes. The QuickBooks bookkeepers make the highest yearly earnings in San Francisco, California. But before quickly packing your bags towards the sunny state, keep in mind the expenses as well. Before shifting your location, always consider the basic expenses and how you will be managing them. It may be possible that you are earning less in one city, but the cost of living is cheaper, and in another city, you might be making more money, but the expenses are equally higher. In the latter case, you end up losing more money. So, always take a well-thought-out and informed decision.

In all, if you are someone good with numbers and have a consistent work ethic, you can very manage to be a QuickBooks bookkeeper. You can even work as a freelance service provider. Providing services is also generally a risk-free approach. The only investment you make is the training you do and the courses you take. After that, all is gain. In this way, you can set your schedule and take up as much work as you can manage. In present times where the future has become unpredictable, freelancing is the way to go.